WAR BONDS

War Bonds

Love Stories From the Greatest Generation

Cindy Hval

CASEMATE
Philadelphia & Oxford

Published in the United States of America and Great Britain in 2015 by
CASEMATE PUBLISHERS
908 Darby Road, Havertown, PA 19083
and
10 Hythe Bridge Street, Oxford, OX1 2EW

ISBN 978-1-61200-290-3
Digital Edition: ISBN 978-1-61200-291-0

Cataloging-in-publication data is available from the Library of Congress and
the British Library.

10 9 8 7 6 5 4 3 2 1

Printed and bound in the United States of America.

For a complete list of Casemate titles please contact:

CASEMATE PUBLISHERS (US)
Telephone (610) 853-9131, Fax (610) 853-9146
E-mail: casemate@casematepublishing.com

CASEMATE PUBLISHERS (UK)
Telephone (01865) 241249, Fax (01865) 794449
E-mail: casemate-uk@casematepublishing.co.uk

Unless otherwise noted, all current photos by Cindy Hval.

CONTENTS

For Derek

Our love story is my favorite one of all.
And for Ethan, Alexander, Zachary and Sam.
My greatest wish is for each of you to find
your own happily ever after.

ACKNOWLEGMENTS

I don't know if it takes a village to write a book, but I do know *War Bonds* would not be possible without the following people.

My parents Tom and Shirley Burnett who showed me happily ever after was possible. I miss you every day, Dad.

Former Spokesman Review editor Tad Brooks who sent me looking for Love Stories back in 2008. Initially, I scoffed and thought *who wants to read Love Stories in a newspaper?* And then I fell in love with writing them and thousands of readers fell in love with reading them.

Author Carol Edgemon Hipperson, who provided invaluable introductions, encouragement and an occasional quiet place to write.

My writer's group who believed I could long before I did: Ruth McHaney Danner, Janet Boehme, Susie Leonard Weller and Jill Barville.

Special thanks to Jill Barville for creating Facebook and blog pages for *War Bonds* and for countless coffee chats and happy hour celebrations—even when the only thing to celebrate was 5 PM.

Undying gratitude to Meg and Mike Andrews and Chuck and Janet Boehme who opened their homes to me and offered what every writer needs most—a quiet place to write.

David Townsend, communications coordinator at Coeur d'Alene Public Library, who suggested the title.

Most of all thank you to the 36 couples featured in *War Bonds*, who shared their wisdom and their memories both painful and pleasant. You opened your minds and your hearts and answered questions that provoked laughter and tears. These are your stories and I have been blessed in hearing and sharing them.

INTRODUCTION

Boy Scouts stood at solemn attention. Teenagers doffed their ball caps. Veterans stood and saluted. Amid the clapping I heard shouts of, "God bless you!" and "We love you," but mostly what I heard were these words shouted over and over again: "Thank you! Thank you for your service."

In May 2010, I was asked to accompany a group of Pearl Harbor survivors during the annual Armed Forces Torchlight Parade in Spokane, Washington. The invitation to ride along stemmed from a series of stories I'd written for the *Spokesman Review* newspaper about the Pearl Harbor Survivors Association.

I was unprepared for the emotional response of the crowd, as the truck carrying the small band of heroes wound its way along the parade route. Seated across from Warren and Betty Schott, I watched them smile and wave at the parade-goers.

The Schotts had been on Ford Island during the attack on Pearl Harbor. While Warren's naval service was noteworthy, it was the story I'd written about their seven-decade marriage that garnered the attention of newspaper readers.

In fact, each time I featured a World War II-era couple in my *Love Stories* series, my inbox overflowed with reader feedback.

"What if you compiled all those stories in a book?" my husband, Derek, asked. "People can't get enough of them."

As I watched the crowd's reaction at the parade that night, I realized he was right. The stories of couples who met or married during or shortly after World War II were compelling—and time was running out to tell them.

The idea for the book percolated while I thought of another couple I'd interviewed, Jerry and Nancy Gleesing.

As a young pilot during WWII, Jerry and his crew had been shot down over Hungary on their second mission and taken captive. Days of fear and uncertainty followed, but when a POW guard gestured for Gleesing to remove his wedding ring, Gleesing found his voice and his courage.

Often during the interview process, things came up that the couples have never shared before—sometimes even with each other.

Take, for example Walter Stewart. His wife, Laura, gave birth to a baby girl who lived only minutes, just before Walter, a sailor, shipped out overseas. As he processed the loss of their child, Walter said, "I sat at the aircraft factory and cried like a baby. You plan for nine months and then it's just gone."

Seventy years later, Laura had looked at him, astonished. "You never told me you cried," she said. "I never knew that."

The stories in War Bonds were born out of the hardship, separation and deprivation of World War II. While the stories still resonate, modern relationships have changed. A half-century from now, it will be difficult to find marriages that have endured 60 to 70 years.

And the passing of approximately 555 World War II veterans each day means that unless documented, their stories die with them.

War Bonds isn't a marriage manual, but as you read these stories, you may be challenged and inspired to cultivate and nurture your own relationships. I know I have been.

As World War II bride Barbara Anderson said, "People today give up too soon. The best is yet to come."

CHAPTER 1
BAND OF GOLD

JERRY AND NANCY
GLEESING, A FEW
DAYS AFTER THEIR
WEDDING.

🌿 *There's a Star Spangled Banner Waving Somewhere*
—PAUL ROBERTS & SHELBY DARNELL, 1942

The thin gold ring on Jerry Gleesing's finger isn't flashy, but he wouldn't trade it for a diamond-studded platinum band. It's rested on that finger since his bride, Nancy, placed it there on June 1, 1944.

It hadn't been easy to win her hand, or even get her to glance his way. In 1940, Jerry heard a new girl had moved to his hometown of LaMoure, North Dakota, and he kept his eyes peeled. There wasn't much excitement in the small town, so the arrival of a young lady was big news. Jerry first spotted her on his way to the ballpark on a Sunday afternoon. Her dark hair and dimples captivated him.

"I was 15," Gleesing recalled. "Quite a bit older than she—I was born in August, Nancy in September." Alas, his status of older man by a month failed to impress the new girl. "She didn't even speak to me for the first six months," he said, shaking his head. "She was a lot smarter than I thought she was." But Jerry was smitten and persistent. By their senior year, they were an "item." Nancy recalled their first date with a smile. "He brought me violets."

In fact, one of their dates became legendary at their small school. "We skipped school one day and had our pictures taken," Nancy said. "We got caught." As a result, when the entire school went on a field trip, Jerry and Nancy were the only two left behind. They didn't mind. Years later at a high school reunion, the day Nancy and Jerry skipped school was still a hot topic.

In 1942, Jerry, 18, enlisted in the Army Air Force and left for basic training. Though she missed him, Nancy shrugged and said, "I knew it was something he had to do." While he went through basic training and then on to flight school, she joined the Army Nurses Corps and served for six months.

"We got married when I got my wings," Jerry recalled. They used his two-week leave for a honeymoon. Soon their first child was on the way. While the war raged in Europe, the couple took comfort in dreaming about their baby. They were sure it would be a son. "We were having Michael," Nancy said, as she remembered that time.

All too quickly, Jerry received orders to deploy to Italy as a flight officer with the 15th Air Force, 459th Bomb Group. He had to leave his wife and

unborn child behind. "It was hard," Nancy admitted. Those three words can't begin to convey the sadness she felt when she kissed him goodbye.

In Europe, things didn't go well for her husband. On Jan. 15, 1945, Jerry said, "I was shot down on my second mission. We nursed the plane along until we got to Hungary." He and his crew had to bail out. Jerry laughed, describing the novelty of his situation. "We never learned how to bail out, just how to fly the plane!"

FLYBOY JERRY
GLEESING, 1943.

He got out of his chute and ran for the trees. "I just had a few seconds to decide how I was going to elude capture." That wasn't enough time. Within minutes he and his crew were surrounded by locals armed with pick-axes and shovels. "I thought they were going to kill us," he said. But instead they quickly handed the captives over to the Germans.

JERRY GLEESING'S FLIGHT CREW, DECEMBER 1944.
Jerry back row, second from left.

Jerry will never forget that first night of captivity. "They lined us up on one side of the courtyard. Five German soldiers with guns stood opposite—you didn't know whether they were going to use those guns." He paused and cleared his throat before continuing the story. "I did pray. I prayed for Michael," he said referring to his unborn child.

Meanwhile, back in North Dakota, Nancy grew worried. "The letters stopped on January 5," she said. For 10 days there was no word. Then a telegram arrived, reporting Jerry as missing in action. She prepared for their child's birth, not knowing her husband's fate.

Jerry had been taken to a prison camp, and as he was being processed, the guard pointed to his wedding ring and motioned for Jerry to remove it. But after days of uncertainty and fear, that was where Jerry drew the line.

"You get to the point where the initial fear is gone," he said. "Whatever happens, happens. I didn't give up my wedding ring. I said, 'I vowed to never take it off. I'm not taking it off.'" The guard stared at him and motioned again for the ring. Jerry simply shook his head. "They let me keep it," he said.

In February 1945 Nancy gave birth to a daughter. "Turns out it wasn't Michael, it was Mary Jean," she said, smiling. In those days babies were taken from their mothers and cared for in the hospital nursery. "I guess I did a little bit of crying," Nancy admitted. The doctor admonished the nurses, "Don't you read the newspaper? Her husband is MIA. You give her that baby any time she wants." So Nancy cuddled her daughter and whispered to her about her brave and handsome father. She promised her baby that Daddy would be home soon.

After three and a half months as a prisoner of war, Jerry's camp at Mooseburg, Germany was liberated. "We saw the tanks come over the hill," he recalled. "Everyone was whooping and hollering. Then the American flag was raised, and it was dead silent." His voice broke. "It was like coming home."

And come home he did, just in time to celebrate their first wedding anniversary. He was asked if he'd like to continue his military service. "They asked me if I wanted to stay in or get out. It took half a second to say 'out,'" he recalled. So instead, he used the GI Bill and graduated from North Dakota State University. He taught agricultural education at a local high school for several years. Then he moved on to a career with a commercial agriculture firm.

Jerry and Nancy raised seven children and were active in their local Catholic parish. Yet the Gleesings would be the first to tell you the course of their true love has had its share of turbulence. As they talked about their six decades together, they debated details, times and places. "We argue a lot for some reason,"

JERRY GLEESING 3 DAYS AFTER HIS WEDDING, 1944.

Jerry said. And across the room Nancy stuck her tongue out at him.

But though they may squabble, the vows they took all those years ago hold firm. "There's something about a commitment," said Jerry. He looked down at his left hand. The sun glinted off the narrow gold band. "It's still there," he said. "I've never taken it off."

LOVE LESSON
"Some days it feels like it all went too fast."—Jerry Gleesing

---

JERRY AND NANCY GLEESING 2010.
Photo courtesy Bart Rayniak, Spokesman Review

*Jerry Gleesing died April 25, 2010. Nancy now wears
his ring on a chain around her neck.*

CHAPTER 2
LADY IN WAITING

DONNA, 1943. THIS
PHOTO IS THE ONLY
ITEM THAT WASN'T
DESTROYED WHEN AN
ARTILLERY BLAST HIT
THE TENT THAT MILT
WAS STANDING IN.

You're No Angel — FRANCIS E. TUCHET, 1942

Donna Stafford first saw her future husband, Milt, in the summer of 1942. As she and her two aunts walked down the sidewalk, they saw a tall, skinny young man walking toward them. "I should have known what I was getting into because he was walking with a .22 slung over his shoulders," she recalled. Shaking her head, she sighed. "I used to hate the months of October and November because he was always gone hunting."

But hunting was the last thing on her mind that sunny afternoon. And once Milt spotted her, hunting was the last thing on his mind, too. "I told my friend, 'I just got to find out who she is—she's a nice looking chick,'" he said, with a chuckle.

Soon after that fateful sidewalk sighting, family members formally introduced Milt and Donna. It didn't take long until the two were spending most of their free time together—seeing movies or hiking through the nearby woods around beautiful Lake Coeur d'Alene.

Milt had dropped out of school to work at the Atlas Mill and as World War II heated up, his boss asked for a 30-day deferment for the hard working young man. When that one expired, he asked for another deferment. But in January 1943, Milt told his boss, "I gotta go sooner or later, so I might as well go, now." He then found himself and 90 other young men from the area boarding a train, intent on letting the Army make soldiers out of loggers, miners and farm kids. After basic training in Utah, Milt discovered to his dismay that he was the only fellow from that group to be sent to Fort Sill, Oklahoma.

On July 4, the kid who'd never set foot outside of Idaho landed in Africa. He missed Donna. He missed his Mom and he missed the pine-shrouded lakes of home. Tucked inside his barracks bag was a picture of the girl he'd left behind. Milt said, "My buddy, Willard, asked, 'Who's that?' I told him, 'That's the girl I'm going to marry.'"

Willard shook his head. "She's too good looking for you. She'll never wait for you!"

He didn't have much time to worry about whether or not Donna would wait for him. Milt and his unit were on the move, traveling to Tunisia with the Third Army, Third Division, under the leadership of General George S. Patton. There, they prepared for the invasion of Sicily. "It was my first round of combat," he said. "The first time I saw dead soldiers." He paused, swallowed hard and looked out the window. "I saw a lot of stuff I didn't want to see."

He described that initial foray into combat as "hell on wheels." The confusion of the nighttime invasion, the shrieking of the shells and the cries of the wounded made a lasting impression. "It scared the hell out of us," he said. "I knew I was in trouble." The problem was that the Germans had taken the high ground and could see the soldiers

MILT STAFFORD (LEFT), AND BUDDY GETTING READY TO MAKE COFFEE, ITALY, 1944.

MILT AND BUDDIES WITH LITTLE ITALIAN GIRL, 1944.

advancing. "They were always shooting down on us!"

From Sicily they battled through Italy. And Milt made a new friend along the way, a dog they named Pinochle. "That dog could tell when the Germans were going to fire an artillery shell," Milt recalled. "She'd run into a foxhole and sure enough, shells would land near us or explode over us." The men quickly learned to follow Pinochle's lead.

But Pinochle wasn't around one afternoon in 1944. Milt had ended up on cooking duty when their cook went AWOL. "He stole an officer's jeep," Milt recalled. "We never did find him. For all I know he's still driving around Italy. I told them I'd taken home ec in high school and that was my downfall. I ended up cooking all the way through Italy."

While he was talking to the first sergeant in the cook tent, the Germans fired a smoke shell over them. Milt told the sergeant they were about to be under artillery fire. There was no time to take cover, and minutes later the sergeant was dead. The blast picked Milt up and tossed him through the air. A friend ran over, grabbed him and pulled him into a foxhole.

MILT AND BUDDIES WITH PINOCHLE, THE DOG. HIS
FRIEND, WILLARD, IS HOLDING THE LITTLE GIRL, 1944.

He spent two days in the field hospital recovering from wounds to his back, which had been torn up by shrapnel. "Some colonel came in and said, 'Can you move your toes?' And like a fool I said, yeah. 'Good,' he said, 'you can go back to the front.'" And back to the front he went. His duffle bag and its contents had been torn to pieces, but one thing remained undamaged: his picture of Donna.

Pinochle wasn't the only Italian friend Milt made. One afternoon a little girl, probably three or four, wandered into their camp. "Her parents had been killed by the Germans and she came to the camp begging for food," Milt said. The locals said she had no family, so Milt and his buddy Willard "adopted" her. They fed her, clothed her and when the shelling started (which it did most every day) they made sure she was in the foxhole with them. They never knew her name.

The Third Division was headed to the Italian Alps when the war ended, and while Milt would have liked to see Switzerland, he said, "I'd seen all of Italy I wanted." When they reached Milan, Milt took the little girl to the US

Embassy, having heard that she might have family in the area. Parting with her proved wrenching. Seventy years later, while looking at pictures of the girl, he covered his face with his hands and tears rolled down his cheeks.

"I never saw her again," he said. "But I think about her every day. I wonder did she find a family? Is she alive?"

Though he worried about the girl, he also couldn't wait to get home. "I had enough points to get out, but my name didn't come up for some reason," he said with a shrug. "I wasn't happy, but the Army doesn't care if you're happy."

Letters from Donna kept his spirits up until finally, in November 1945, Milt made it home—but not before he said another sad goodbye. He'd hoped to take Pinochle with him, but the dog wasn't allowed to board the ship. A little girl had been playing with Pinochle while Milt tried to get the dog on board. When he realized his quest was in vain, he gave the little girl Pinochle's lead. She beamed and hugged both Milt and the dog, and he felt confident that his furry friend had found a good home.

MILT AND PINOCHLE, THE DOG HE HAD TO LEAVE BEHIND. ITALY, 1944.

After surviving a horrific storm in the Atlantic and a snowstorm in Montana, a bus finally dropped the exhausted soldier off in his hometown. At 3 am, he walked to his mother's house and let himself in through the unlocked door. Hungry like always, he had made his way to the kitchen when he heard his mother yell, "Who is that?"

Milt hollered back, "It's me, Ma. I finally got home!"

While under fire and frightened for his life, Milt said he prayed to God to live, and prayed to see his Mama again. He said, "I must have prayed to see my mom at least 15 times, but she never showed up!" That middle-of-the-night kitchen reunion was a celebration for both of them.

You would think that after arriving

home at last, the young soldier would have had his sweetheart on his mind, but all Milt could think about was hunting. "My uncle promised me if I got back before hunting season was over, he'd take me to Priest Lake," Milt said. Then he shrugged. "I made it back two days before the season closed."

After his hunting excursion, he and Donna were reunited, but their courtship was tumultuous. They got engaged, but soon broke up. "It was my fault," Milt admits. Donna said he was possessive and resented her independence. When he constantly questioned her comings and goings, she said, "I told him to forget it and broke up with him."

The break up didn't last long. They worked out their differences and on March 10, 1948 they were married at the Hitching Post, a local wedding chapel. Not long after, Willard came to visit them. Milt introduced him to Donna and exulted, "Well, here she is, you old SOB!" Willard laughed and congratulated him.

Milt returned to his job at the Atlas Mill, earning 32 cents an hour. He worked there for 43 years before retiring. On his meager income, they bought a car, rented an apartment and settled into married life. Or tried to. "I was still hunting and fishing every weekend," said Milt.

"It took a long time to cure him," Donna said.

Soon, their first daughter was born, followed seven years later by another. Having his own daughters soothed some of the sadness Milt felt about the little girl he'd left in Italy.

In addition to outdoor activities, Milt was an avid baseball player and for many years played catcher and first base for the Coeur d'Alene Lakesiders club. "We had a hell of a team," he said. His wife grew to love the game, too. After they retired they traveled to the Baseball Hall of Fame. "I was more excited than he was," Donna said, smiling.

Donna worked at City Hall for a time and eventually became a member of the "if-you-can't-beat-'em-join-'em" club. "I finally learned to like fishing," she said. "In fact, I loved it." For many years the couple had a lakefront cabin. "He'd get in the boat and be gone for hours," Donna recalled. "I thought if I ever want to see him, I'd better find out what this fishing stuff is all about. Then I was the one who didn't want to quit. And sometimes I out-fished him!"

"She didn't out-fish me too many times, I'll tell you that!" Milt interrupted.

For 66 years the Staffords have worked out their differences with grit and a healthy dose of humor. "I wanted to buy her a rifle," Milt said. "She told me, 'You'd be the first thing I shot with it!'" He paused and grinned. "So I didn't buy it."

His wife smiled, too. "I guess I could be ornery, every once in a while."

Milt freely admits his husbandly skills were lacking at times. "I had some stupid ways about me. She had a lot of opportunity to tell me to hit the road, but thank God, she didn't."

LOVE LESSON

"Pay attention! Marriage is a two-way street. It isn't all about your way and it isn't all about her way. It's the together that counts." — Milt Stafford

---

MILT AND DONNA STAFFORD, 2010.

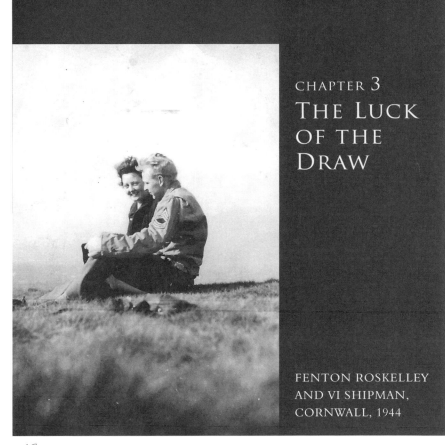

CHAPTER 3

THE LUCK
OF THE
DRAW

FENTON ROSKELLEY
AND VI SHIPMAN,
CORNWALL, 1944

🌿 *Sentimental Journey*
—LES BROWN, BEN HOMER & ARTHUR GREEN, 1944

Aslip of paper drawn at random from a hat led to happily ever after for Fenton and Violet Roskelley.

Violet, from Yorkshire, England had been drafted into the British ATS (Auxiliary Territorial Service) in 1943. She wasn't pleased about it, feeling the army was no place for a properly raised British girl. Because of the war, brash, young American soldiers were everywhere, and the British girls were crazy about them.

But not Violet.

"I told my sister, Betty, 'Don't get mixed up with an American,'" she recalled. "They were a little too friendly for me."

The apple-cheeked beauty worked in communications at a command post in Cornwall. "The battery was stationed on a cliff overlooking the sea," she said. "German bombers flew over us, but fortunately the bombs they dropped ended up in the sea!"

One day a message arrived requesting an operator at regimental headquarters. In the interest of fairness, Violet suggested they put all 12 operators' names in a hat and draw one to see who would have to be transferred. Violet reached in and drew out a slip of paper. To her dismay she drew her own name. "I was very upset. I didn't want to leave all my friends," she said. But, off she went to headquarters at Penhale House in Cornwall.

One afternoon in May 1944 she decided to take a walk to the sea, its beauty marred only by the barrage balloons that floated overhead. "Along comes this good-looking American," she said. He offered a friendly greeting and asked if he could accompany her. "Right away I realized he was intelligent. We just talked and visited, and then he asked if he could see me again."

The soldier was Fenton Roskelley from Challis, Idaho. He'd graduated from the University of Idaho in 1938 with a degree in journalism, proud that he'd written the most column inches for the college newspaper. In 1940 he was hired as a copy editor and beat reporter for the *Spokane Daily Chronicle*, earning $18 a week. He loved the work, but duty called. Fenton was drafted into the Army in 1942. Assigned to the 776th Liberty Bell anti-aircraft battalion, he soon set sail for England. "My outfit was attached to her regiment," he said.

VIOLET SHIPMAN, 1943.

Fenton vividly remembers that first meeting. "I knew the type of girl she was from our first conversation. I knew instantly that she was the girl for me."

For Violet, meeting Ross—as she called him—shattered her preconceived notions about Americans. "I thought his name was Ross Kelley, so I've always called him Ross," she said, laughing. But she grew serious as she gazed at him. "He was a gentleman, educated, everything a girl could want," she said. Then she grinned. "Despite the fact that he was an American."

He courted her with long walks

in the countryside, dart games at the local canteen and K-rations. "I loved to eat the chocolate out of the rations," Violet said. "It wasn't great chocolate, but it was more than we had at the time."

Soon Fenton got word that he was being shipped out. Before he left he asked Violet if she would agree to be engaged. They'd known each other just six weeks. "I couldn't imagine living in America where the gangsters are!" she said. "England was my whole world. I'd never even thought about marrying an American!"

Still, before he left she agreed to the engagement. The couple kept in touch by mail, as Fenton went to Paris and then to Germany. He grinned: "I was living in foxholes. I had nothing better to do than to write letters." Those missives meant everything to his sweetheart. "I still have every letter he wrote me," Violet said.

She had been sent to Kent. "It was scary in Seven Oakes," she said. "Every night V-rockets would come over. Fortunately none hit our area." The rockets went on to London where they destroyed both buildings and people.

One day she got a telegram from her mother. It read, "Violet, you'd better get leave. Ross is coming home to marry you." Shaking her head, Violet said, "So, I got a 10-day leave and went home to Yorkshire." She hastily made arrangements for the wedding.

Meanwhile, in Germany, Fenton also made wedding preparations. "For the first time in my life, I used the black market," he said. He gathered cigarettes and sugar to barter. "I wanted my bride to have a good honeymoon, and I wanted to have money to spend on her." He collected the equivalent of $500 and presented it to Violet. He chuckled. "She'd never seen so much money in her life!"

They married on March 23, 1945 in a small church. Both wore their uniforms. Violet's regiment had one wedding dress that they shared among them. She shuddered, "I could have worn the regimental wedding dress, but everyone else had worn that." She didn't have much of trousseau, either. "I'd given away most of my clothes because I thought I'd be in the Army forever."

On their honeymoon the realities of marriage set in for her new husband. "I had to go shopping with her," he said, raising his shoulders. "I've never liked shopping." Violet got an eye-opener herself, when her new husband tipped a cab driver with a one-pound note, instead of the customary

10 shillings. "I took charge of the money after that." She found the American penchant for taking cabs, bewildering. "They would never take a bus. They spent more money on taxis than I made in a week!"

When their honeymoon ended, Fenton returned to duty in Germany. He'd been asked to set up a journalism school and publish a paper for the troops in Allied-occupied Germany. The paper was called *The Rhine Valley News.* He considered the project the most satisfying accomplishment of his military career. Almost 60 years later, he was baffled to find no mention of *The Rhine Valley News* during Internet searches.

Twelve American sergeants had operated a unique, first-of-its-kind journalism school for budding reporters and would-be linotype and press operators for two months in Heidelberg after the end of the war. They published two newspapers for thousands of soldiers, as well as brigade and battalion histories. "But it doesn't even rate a hit on Google," he said. All that remains of the groundbreaking project resides in an old suitcase in Fenton's basement—a few dozen fading copies of *The Rhine Valley News.* While he relished the work, he missed his bride. In August of 1945 they enjoyed a brief reunion before Fenton was shipped home with his unit. He returned to his civilian job at the *Daily Chronicle* and waited for his wife to join him.

In April 1946 Violet endured an arduous 14-day crossing to America on the H.M.S. *Huddleston.* "I was seasick the entire time," she sighed. The

ROSKELLEY WEDDING, 1945.

FENTON ROSKELLY, MILITARY JOURNALISM SCHOOL, 1945.
ROSKELLY IS AT FAR LEFT, BENDING OVER DESK.

ship's newspaper had a headline that read, "Muddling Across the Puddle on the Huddle. Columbus did it faster and he had sails."

While aboard ship, she was awakened every morning by the song, *Sentimental Journey.* "I couldn't listen to that tune for a long time," she said.

Once off the ship she boarded a train in Chicago for a weeklong journey to Spokane, arriving in the city at night. Violet had endured London black-outs for so long, the sight of the city rolling out before her, glittering with lights, took her breath away. She said, "It looked like a fairyland. I'd never seen anything more beautiful in my life." Her handsome husband was there to greet her when she arrived. "I've never regretted bringing my bride over," he said. "I was so happy to see her!"

And her fairyland came complete with a little yellow house and a white picket fence. Daughter, Patricia, arrived in 1947, followed by son, John, in 1948.

Violet embraced her new homeland and became an American citizen in 1949. "You can tell she lost her accent," Fenton teased. She wasn't the only one taking citizenship classes in 1949. "There were lots of us British

ROSKELLEY SNAPPED
THIS PHOTO OF 3
FAMOUS GENERALS
IN GERMANY, 1945.
FROM LEFT TO RIGHT,
PATTON, BRADLEY,
AND EISENHOWER.

girls taking the class," she said. In fact, her children remember many gatherings of the "English Ladies."

Violet was happy with two children, but in 1960, a daughter, Heather, surprised them. "It was a wonderful thing!" she said.

Fenton was an outdoor writer, editor and reporter for Spokane newspapers for more than 60 years. There isn't a river or stream in the great northwest he didn't walk and cast a fly from its banks; nor a lake he didn't know the depth to the inch. He never missed a day of work, writing as many as six stories or columns a week. Of course, fishing and hunting was part of his job description.

In 1986, the couple returned to England as guests of the British tourism department. Violet said, "It was odd to be a 'guest' in my home country!"

When asked to what he attributes the longevity of their marriage, Fenton grinned at his wife and replied, "I married the type of woman who doesn't like change." Violet returned his smile. "My husband is handsome, intelligent, thoughtful, a good provider. What more could a girl want?"

Nothing.

The couple is well aware of the part luck plays in their story. A story made possible by a slip of paper, drawn from a hat.

LOVE LESSON

"I've always been one to stick with people. Once I decided Vi was the one I loved, that was it."— Fenton Roskelley

---

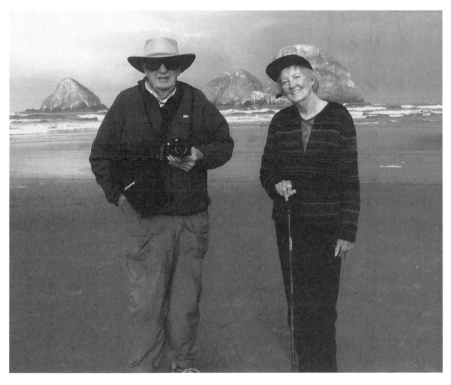

ROSKELLYS ON THE OREGON COAST, 2010. *Photo courtesy of the family.*

Violet Roskelley died July 27, 2012
Fenton Roskelley died January 30, 2013

CHAPTER 4

HAVE A LITTLE FAITH

JOHN JASLEY, FLIGHT
SCHOOL, 1943.

JOHN AND CHRISTINE,
DATING, 1944.

🌿 *Pennsylvania Polka*— LESTER LEE & ZEKE MANNERS, 1942

A s the first strains of the Pennsylvania Polka drifted out onto the dance floor, Christine Seibert's partner looked down at her, dismayed. "I don't dance the polka, do you?" the soldier asked.

"Why, yes, I do," she replied. The G.I. pondered the situation as they sat the dance out. Finally, he said, "I've got a buddy who can dance the polka; will you be here next week?"

"Sure," she said, and promptly forgot the conversation.

But the solider was true to his word. The next Saturday he and his buddy, John Jasley, were waiting for her. John remembers the day well. "It was October 24, 1942 in Jacksonville, Florida," he said, smiling. When the band fired up a polka, Christine and John danced and continued dancing throughout the evening. During a lull in the music, he turned to his dance partner and said, "Close your eyes and hold out your hands."

Christine wasn't sure what he was up to. "I thought I was going to get a cockroach or a mouse!" Still, she did as he asked. She was pleasantly surprised. "He put a little box of candy in my hand," she said.

John grinned at her from across the room. "She saved that candy until it turned white."

The young soldier from New Jersey had enlisted in the Army Air Corps immediately after the bombing of Pearl Harbor and was trained as both a gunner and a radio operator. Shortly after basic training, his First Sergeant entered the barracks and barked, "Can any of you guys type?" John admitted he'd taken a typing course in high school. "They put me in the office," he said. But soon the First Sergeant had another frustration—no one in the unit could pass the gunnery test. "Oh, I can pass that test," John said. So off he went to gunnery school.

His training complete, he was ready to make time for the lovely Christine. After the dance, he invited her to see a movie the following week. She agreed. A few days later, he took the bus to her house and arrived early to find her dad waiting for him. Her father was reading the Wall Street Journal and asked John's opinion about various stocks and bonds. John shook his head. "I was a Depression-era kid who knew nothing about stocks." However, he quickly decided to learn. "The next time he asked me I was going to know something," he said.

John had already decided Christine was an investment worth making. After their date, her father asked, "So, what did you think of that guy?" Knowing if she told him how much she liked John, her protective dad would find fault with him, Christine feigned nonchalance. She shrugged. "Oh, he's okay."

Her father replied, "Well, he seemed to have more brains that most of the fellows you've been bringing around."

Christine's mother encouraged her to invite John for Thanksgiving dinner. Later, Christine found out he'd been accepted to flight school, but cancelled his application so he could spend the holiday with her. "He told me he didn't want to leave me, because he wasn't sure I'd be there when he got back," she recalled. At Christmas he arrived for dinner bearing gifts: razor blades for her dad and coffee for her mom—items hard to come by due to rationing. "My mom couldn't get by on the coffee rations so he brought her five pounds of coffee from the mess hall!"

What he wanted to give Christine was an engagement ring. But when he told her he wanted to marry her, she replied, "Oh no you don't!"

She explained her reluctance, "He was Catholic and I was Protestant. I didn't want him to give up his faith, and I didn't want to be Catholic." In addition, they knew that John, who by then had completed flight school, would soon be sent overseas. Unlike many wartime couples, they didn't want to marry, only to be separated. "If something happened to me over there—well, I didn't want her to be saddled with that," said John.

And the ever-practical Christine said, "We didn't want to have a baby and then be apart." Eventually, she accepted his proposal and promised to wait for his return. She asked him to write her dad a letter requesting permission to marry.

John shook his head. The task proved daunting. "My wastepaper basket was full of all the ones I tried to write."

JOHN JASLEY, 1944.

In March 1943 he shipped out to Italy. "I only had to fly 35 missions to get to go home, but I flew 50," he said. "Some of them were 'mulligans,'—training missions—but we still got shot at." On one memorable mission John's crew returned to base with 640 holes in their B-24. "They shot us up real bad," he recalled. As he inspected his gear he noticed a tear in his parachute. "A hot piece of flak had gone through my vest, into my chute and fused into the nylon." He still has that piece of flak—a reminder of the dangers he survived.

Others weren't as fortunate. He shrugged and said, "Thirty-six went over in my group and only three came back."

One day Christine received a letter from John. "Samson got it," John wrote. And that's how she found out a mutual friend had been killed.

John looked down his hands and sighed. "Samson's airplane blew up."

John didn't escape without injury. He earned a purple heart when a piece of flak pierced his flight suit on a mission. "I looked down and my leg was covered in blood," he recalled. "When we landed, they pulled the flak out with a pair of tweezers." In addition to his other duties, John served as a photographer. When they flew out of Italy, he took pictures of bridges, factories and railroad stations—photos that provided vital information for the Allies.

Finally, in October 1944 Christine got a call from a stevedore on transport ship. "A rough voice said, 'Your boyfriend is home,'" she recalled. "I said, 'Who are you?' And he said, 'What the hell do you care? Your boyfriend's home!'"

JASLEY WEDDING PHOTO, NOVEMBER 1944.

One month later, on November 16, they married. When asked how they resolved the issue of their conflicting religious backgrounds, Christine replied, "We didn't." While John was facing imminent peril overseas, he said he realized everyone—Catholic and Protestant alike—prayed to the same God. Unfortunately, their families weren't as open-minded. John's family was so appalled that he wanted to marry a Protestant that they wouldn't allow his brother to be in the wedding.

When John was discharged he accepted a job with National Cash Register in Reno, Nevada, far away from both sets of parents. "We were afraid they'd interfere," said Christine. The couple believes that that long-ago decision, to live at a distance from their parents, contributed to the success of their union.

As they settled into married life, John rarely spoke of his combat experience. Christine said, "He'd lost all his friends—he just wanted to forget."

In 1946 Christine gave birth to a daughter and three years later, a son. Sadly, the baby boy lived only one day. "That was the most difficult time of our lives," said John. But they coped with their grief together and took delight in their daughter.

John worked for National Cash Register for 36 years before retiring at 62. Since that time, the couple brought together by the Pennsylvania Polka has made time for dancing, wine tasting and travel. And 16 years ago, their conflict of faith question was finally resolved.

"Our grandson was marrying a Catholic girl and we sat next to the priest at the rehearsal dinner," Christine said. She and John told him that when they wed in 1944, they hadn't been allowed to marry in the Church.

"Things are much different now," the priest said, and promptly offered to marry them the following morning before their grandson's wedding. Fifty-three years after their first wedding, they were finally married by a priest. When John called his mother to tell her the news, he said, "She was so happy she cried."

At 95, they've both slowed down a bit. But their love and appreciation for the life they've built hasn't dimmed. Christine smiled. "He tells me every day that I'm the best thing that ever happened to him."

LOVE LESSON

"The best thing we ever did was move far away from our parents."
— Christine Jasley

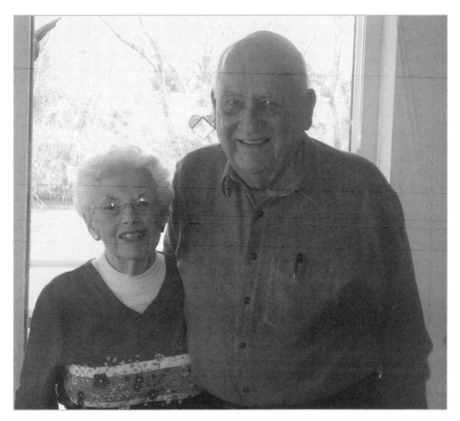

THE JASLEYS, 2010.

CHAPTER 5
FOOTLOOSE, FANCY FREE AND FUN

WAYE AND CLARA BEST WEDDING, APRIL 2, 1942.

🌿 *Ac-Cent-Tchu-Ate the Positive*
— HAROLD ARLEN & JOHNNY MERCER, 1944

Wayne Best is clear about who is to blame for a union that spanned 71 years. "It was all Clara's fault that we met!" he said. Holding hands as they sat close to each other, they recalled their first date on July 4, 1941. Clara had been invited to accompany friends to Coeur d'Alene, Idaho for the Independence Day festivities; however, her boyfriend had to work. Wayne grinned. "But I was footloose and fancy free."

With her boyfriend's okay, she joined Wayne and their mutual friends. "We drove to Coeur d'Alene and got hamburgers and milkshakes and sat on the curb," said Clara, describing their al fresco meal. Wayne was so impressed by the brunette beauty that he immediately tried to make plans to see her again. Clara was a popular girl, but Wayne was undeterred by her elusiveness, and he persisted. Clara nudged his shoulder with hers. "He asked me out three times before I was available."

After that Wayne made sure to secure another date with her before he took her home. In fact, he kept her so busy Clara said, "I finally had to break up with my boyfriend."

Wayne had served a four-year boilermaker apprenticeship at a welding company when the pair met. "Every now and then the soot would flare up around you—in those days they didn't have a lot of what you'd call safety measures," Wayne said. "I gave up being a boilermaker and became a combination welder."

Clara's work wasn't quite as dangerous. "I had a job taking care of two boys from a wealthy family," she said. "I learned how to ride a bike and roller skate with those boys."

When asked how they became engaged, Wayne replied, "Well, I had to wait quite awhile for her to ask me." Clara shook her head and laughed, but they agreed that the engagement occurred in December 1941. Before the couple set a wedding date, they had an obstacle to overcome. "She was Catholic and I was Protestant," said Wayne. "We agreed that I would take lessons and we'd be married in the Catholic Church."

On December 6, Wayne and his brother took a bus to Seattle to watch the Washington State University vs. Texas A&M game in Tacoma. After the game, his brother returned home, but Wayne remained and went out on the town with a friend. "We slept in the next morning and when we finally went out, they said, 'Did you hear what happened? Pearl Harbor was bombed!'"

Instead of returning home, Wayne took a job at a shipyard on Harbor Island. He looked up the nearest Catholic Church and met with the priest to continue his instruction. "We visited and the priest said, 'I think you've gone far enough. I wouldn't have any problem marrying you.'"

Clara interjected, "Then they talked about sports!"

Wayne bought his fiancée a $26 airline ticket so she could fly to Seattle and make the wedding arrangements. "I didn't want her to spend the night on bus or train," he said.

The couple married in the parish parlor on April 26, 1942. One wedding photo in particular captures their sense of fun, showing Clara holding a chain that's wrapped around Wayne's waist. "I guess somebody figured she needed a little help," said Wayne.

Their honeymoon was rather unconventional, as well. After their wedding night in a Seattle hotel, Clara and her bridal party set off for Canada.

"The girls had never been to British Columbia," she explained "We stayed two or three days."

Meanwhile, the draft board had lost track of Wayne. "I didn't file a change of address, when I moved," he explained. "When they caught up with me, it was no more deferments even though I worked in the ship-yards." He shrugged. "I just figured it was meant to be." So he reported to Ft. Lewis and was sent to Louisiana for basic training.

Clara, newly pregnant, returned to Spokane to live with her family. She admitted the separation was wrenching. "It was hard to take, but it was work that had to be done."

WAYNE BEST, 1943.

And it was hard work. "I was assigned to the Third Armored Signal Battalion," said Wayne. "I was the head of the wire team that laid telephone lines. I made staff sergeant in a year and a half." Before he was sent overseas he learned he had a son, Gordon Wayne, born May 23, 1943. "I got to come home on leave that summer," Wayne said. His son would be three before he saw him again.

After a short stint in Hawaii, Wayne boarded a ship and set sail for Okinawa. "I got to see a very big portion of the Pacific Ocean, as we were at sea for six weeks." He joined his company every morning for ship-board exercises, and when he went ashore with a full field pack and three days of rations, he appreciated those workouts at sea.

Wayne said, "We followed a lot of fighting as we went up the island. The Japanese were still strafing Kadena." Yet he didn't lose any of his wire team. "We lucked out," he said. "The other part of the company lost a couple guys." He grew quiet and glanced out his living room window. "Some parts you don't remember—some parts will be in your mind forever."

Not all memories are painful. "We had the job of cleaning up areas in

Okinawa," Wayne said. "We found all these bottles of what was supposed to be Philippine rum." He laughed. "We traded some of those bottles to the kitchen for cans of Spam." However, his photos show the fellows kept at least a couple of them for their own consumption!

When the Japanese surrendered, his battalion was sent to Korea. While at sea they were hit by a typhoon—an experience Wayne never wants to endure again.

Six months later, in December 1945, he received his discharge. "They offered me a deal to stay in, but I said no." He glanced at Clara. "I had somebody to come home to." He made it home in time for Christmas, and within weeks found a job at American Machine Works where he worked until he retired in 1980.

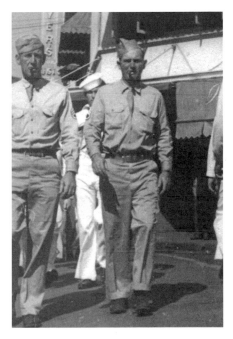

Clara stayed home with Gordon until he was a senior in high school. She then took a job at Old National Bank, starting out as a teller and ending up assistant manager. When she retired after 22 years, she still remembered the name of every person who walked through the doors of her branch.

The couple lived in the home they purchased in 1950 until they moved to a retirement community

WAYNE BEST, RIGHT, HAWAII, 1945.

a few years ago. Reflecting on the longevity of their jobs, home, and marriage, Wayne said, "We've never been in a hurry to move around."

Upon his retirement, Clara bought him a set of golf clubs. "Well, he had to have something to do!" However, she had no desire to "hit that little ball around." That changed when she retired. At 62, she took up golf and found she loved it. For 17 years the couple traveled to Hawaii for golfing vacations, and maintained an active social life.

In June 2011 Wayne and his son took an Honor Flight to Washington, DC, to visit the World War II Memorial. "It was a pleasant trip due to the

WAYNE BEST (BACK ROW MIDDLE), THE DAY
THE GUYS FOUND "PHILIPPINE RUM."

fact that I had my son taking care of me." But then he paused and his eyes filled with tears as he described the Memorial. "Sitting there looking at all the gold stars, made me think of what they've done. . . ."

Brushing off the fact that he, too, did his part for his country, Wayne was happier to talk about his wife. When asked what made their marriage work for seven decades, he said, "It makes it awfully difficult if you have to keep your head down to the grindstone." Then he smiled at Clara, "We weren't afraid to make time for a little fun."

STAFF SGT. WAYNE BEST, 1945.

LOVE LESSON
"We're still very much in love. That's something that has never changed."
—Clara Best

WAYNE AND CLARA BEST, 2011.

Wayne Best died February 18, 2013
Clara Best died May 21, 2013

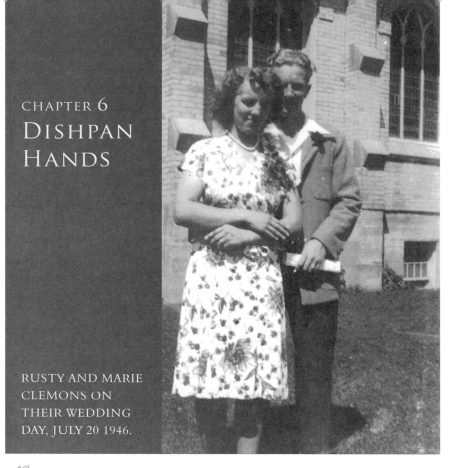

CHAPTER 6

DISHPAN
HANDS

RUSTY AND MARIE
CLEMONS ON
THEIR WEDDING
DAY, JULY 20 1946.

After Hours — AVERY PARRISH, 1940

L
ove can make a person do unexpected things. For Rusty Clemons, it motivated him to wash dishes at his brother's restaurant. It wasn't brotherly love that compelled this act of service—it was a pretty waitress named Marie who caught his eye. One night when the dishwasher didn't show up, Marie offered to pitch in and scrub pots and pans. Rusty quickly volunteered to help her. "I went over to the restaurant a lot to just hang around," Rusty recalled. "I was footloose, you know."

It had been awhile since the 25-year-old young man felt footloose. He'd grown up in tiny Rice, Washington, and times were tough. "I quit high school in my junior year," he said. He joined the Civilian Conservation Corps (CCC) in 1940. "I fought fires and dug ditches for $30 a month and 25 of that went home to the folks."

By August of 1942, Rusty had a new boss. "I got drafted into the Army," he said. He joined a group of other young men, all from small surrounding towns, on a bus that took them to the city. "Some of the guys were loggers, still wearing their boots," he said. Assigned to the 551st Signal Battalion, he shipped out from Catalina with 4,000 other soldiers aboard the USS *Wharton*.

USS
WHARTON

After 30 days at sea, Rusty arrived at his home for the next 15 months—Bougainville Island.

Though the island was in sight, they weren't allowed off the ship because a beachhead hadn't yet been established. "We were out there like sitting ducks for several days." But eventually, with their feet on dry land, the soldiers quickly set up a tent base and dug latrines. Those latrines played a pivotal role in a practical joke played on Rusty.

The facilities consisted of a board with seats cut out, perched over newly dug trenches. Swathes of mosquito netting dangled from the roof, making up the walls and a

RUSTY CLEMONS,
BOUGAINVILLE, 1944.

RUSTY WITH
HIS WEAPON,
BOUGAINVILLE,
1944.

door. One night as Rusty used the latrine, his buddies snuck around in the jungle behind him. One of them grabbed a stick and poked at Rusty's back through the netting. Rusty was sure what he felt was the sharp end of a Japanese bayonet. "I was through the netting and back to camp in seconds," he said. And there he found his buddies grabbing their sides and rolling on the ground with laughter.

His fear, however, was justified. The Japanese-occupied island quickly became a focal point for Allied forces. "We set up radar to keep an eye on enemy planes and to help our own planes go on their missions," Rusty recalled. "Our radar was going 24/7." Even so, he said the biggest enemy he

RUSTY'S
HOME FOR
15 MONTHS,
BOUGAINVILLE,
1944.

faced was jungle rot and malaria, though the malaria didn't hit him until he'd returned to the States.

Due to the urgency of their mission, the troops didn't get time off for extended rest and recreation. However, they did enjoy USO shows with Bob Hope and Jack Benny. Rusty said, "It was a nice break."

From Bougainville, his group went to the Philippines and finally, in December 1945, Rusty had earned enough points return home. "I was gone from home 42 months." Though none of his family knew when he'd return, the first person he saw when he got off the bus in his hometown was his brother, Clem. "I couldn't believe it!" Rusty said. Clem showed Rusty the restaurant he'd purchased, and that's where Marie caught his eye.

"I was in high school and waited on tables in the evening," Marie said. She liked Rusty's friendly manner, but his wavy blond hair really attracted her. "Boy, I wanted to run my fingers through it!" she said. The night her suitor offered to help wash dishes proved pivotal. "We got to holding hands," Rusty said. "I don't know whether it was during the wash or rinse cycle."

With the dishes finished, he offered to walk Marie home. "I fell pretty hard for her," he said, and he's not kidding. It was a bitterly cold January evening. "I went to kiss her good night and we both slipped on the ice and fell down." He shrugged. "I thought it was a good start."

Seeing Marie home became a regular part of Rusty's routine. The night policeman took a liking to the couple and often gave them a ride. Marie worried her parents wouldn't like Rusty because of their seven-year age difference, but her parents quickly accepted him.

"He didn't seem older," she said. "But oh man, I just fell in love with him."

For his part, Rusty said, "I thought she was a cute little trick, but I really didn't have marriage in mind when I met her."

He's still not quite sure what happened—but on July 20, 1946, he married that cute waitress, having sold his prized 1939 Dodge to afford a wife. "I think she might have applied the pressure," he teased. "Because the next thing I knew, there I was at the church!"

Marie just laughed. "Well, I didn't want him to get away!"

Finding steady employment proved difficult. Rusty worked at a service station and drove truck for the County Road Department and later for a local mining company.

In May 1947, Marie gave birth to their first child, Jim. "I was too young to have kids," Marie said, shaking her head. "What was I thinking?" The couple laughed as they recalled their rocky adjustment to parenthood. One night the baby woke and Marie asked Rusty to warm a bottle for him. "While the bottle was warming, I fell asleep on the couch," he said. The bottle warmer boiled dry, the bottle shattered, and the baby was screaming when Marie got up to investigate.

"There was some debate as to whether I could stay around or not," said Rusty, shooting his wife a quick grin. "It took me awhile to get back in her good graces."

Marie shook her head. "I could have killed him!"

Their family grew with the birth of Janet in 1948 and Jerry in 1951. "My folks helped out with the babies," Marie said. "Thank goodness!"

In 1958 they moved to the home they still live in when Rusty took a job driving truck for the Nehi Beverage Company. Unfortunately, Nehi soon cancelled the route and Rusty was out of a job. "I took what work I could get," he said. "I dug ditches, delivered packages . . ." Finally, Rusty got a job at an upscale hotel in the maintenance department, where he worked for 16 years before moving on to a position at the County Court-house.

As for Marie, she likes to say she went back to school—she became a cook for a local school district in 1960. She enjoyed her work, but after 18 years on the job, she found the kitchen innovations unpalatable. "When I started, we peeled our own potatoes and cleaned our own birds," she said. "Things changed so much. It was all prepackaged mixes and foods—I couldn't stand it."

Upon retirement the couple indulged in their favorite pastime. "We loved to camp," Marie said. "When we first started camping it meant taking the bedding off the beds and the pans out of the cupboard. We eventually bought a motor home to go visit the kids."

They say their 68 years of marriage has gone by in a blur. Rusty still shakes his head when he recalls the night they washed dishes together in his brother's restaurant. "I don't have a clue why I did that! I never did like to wash dishes."

Marie smiled at him from across their table. "I couldn't have a better husband," she said. "Every day, even now, is precious."

LOVE LESSON
"The best advice I can give, is look for someone patient and understanding."
—Marie Clemons

RUSTY AND MARIE, 2011.

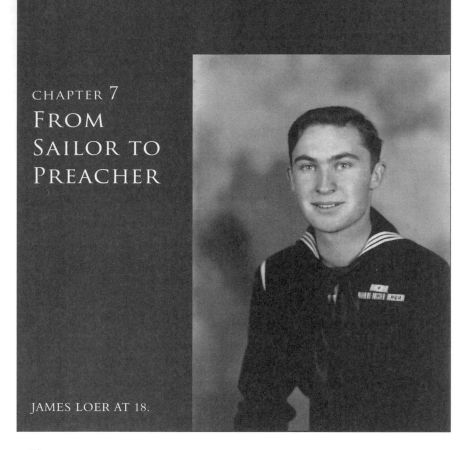

CHAPTER 7

FROM SAILOR TO PREACHER

JAMES LOER AT 18.

🌿 *Beyond the Sea* — CHARLES TRENET & JACK LAWRENCE, 1946

S eventeen-year-old James Loer enlisted in the Navy in January 1941, mainly because he didn't want to be in the Army. "I didn't like the idea of sleeping in a foxhole and eating cold rations," he said. Plus, the adventure of sailing the seas appealed to the North Carolina native. "I wanted to see the world," he said. Then he shook his head and laughed. "I didn't know I'd see it through a porthole!"

However, he did avoid foxholes. "I had a bed and a hot meal every night."

James was enjoying one of those hot meals while stationed in Norfolk, Virginia when the news of the attack on Pearl Harbor came over the loud-speaker. The nation was at war and a young man's wish to cross an ocean or two was about to come true. During the next few years, he logged 250,000 miles aboard the USS *Washington*, a convoy escort battleship. The ship was often under fire by both submarines from below and bombers from above. "Everyone had a battle station," he said, describing his job as gunner's mate.

"Those guns were the first line of defense against enemy air attack."

The screeching of the aircraft is a sound that James has never forgotten. "The plane made a horrible noise when it dove," he said. "They tried to get as close as they could before they released the bombs."

When not actively engaging the enemy, James and his fellow sailors spent time target practicing. One day as he returned from an exercise he walked under the #10 gun. A shell hadn't been released, and just as James walked past, the gun fired. The concussion from the blast knocked him down. "I managed to get up, but I couldn't hear anything."

The young sailor spent two days in sickbay and eventually suffered permanent hearing loss as a result of that close call. Still, he counts himself lucky. The USS *Washington* never received a direct hit though they were under fire repeatedly. "They got all but three of the cargo ships," he said, shrugging.

Accidents claimed lives as well. "One of my better friends was buried as sea," James recalled, and his voice grew husky at the memory. "After a short service we wrapped him up in a canvas bag with a projectile between his legs (for weight) and down he went."

After being discharged in 1946, James returned to North Carolina ready to leave the sailor's life behind. "I'd served four years, eight months and nine days—you really counted the days back then."

He found work in a textile mill, and one afternoon at a church service he spotted a pretty girl named Helen singing in a trio. James, an aspiring minister, had been invited to preach on a Baptist radio program, and the girls were invited to sing. James offered them a ride. Helen glanced across the table at her husband as she recalled that first meeting. "I thought he was handsome," she said.

James shook his head and interrupted. "I can tell you right now this isn't going to be romantic!" But romance can mean many different things. For instance, Helen found it romantic that James "just happened" to sit by her in church Sunday after Sunday. She also liked the way he interacted with boys in the Sunday school class he taught. Every Saturday he took them out to play ball and get an ice cream cone. "I asked Helen if she wanted to go with me," said James. And she did.

They conducted most of their courtship in church. "Well, we did have a picnic one time," Helen recalled.

Soon James left to attend Bible school in Tennessee and their visits were limited to weekends. While they were apart, James spent a lot of time thinking about Helen—wondering if she'd agree to become a preacher's wife. He said he'd always wanted to be a pastor, but after the war he got serious about it. "Young people today handle their lives so carelessly," he said. "When you go through a war you take life a lot more seriously."

HELEN MILLER, 19.

When he came home for Christmas break in December 1947, he asked Helen to marry him as they sat in his Oldsmobile—the one place where they were guaranteed some privacy.

During the war, Helen, at 22, had worked in the fingerprint department of the FBI in Washington, DC. She felt she'd earned the maturity to make this life-altering decision. She agreed to be his wife. However, her father was not pleased that his only daughter chose to marry a preacher. "He said, 'You're going to make your bed hard and you're going to lie in it.'" And the ladies in their church weren't happy, either. "They thought I'd have a big church wedding, but after he asked me, he had to get back to school."

So the couple married on January 18, 1948, in the home of the pastor with a few friends to witness their nuptials. Though they had no honeymoon, Helen said, "We ended up traveling a lot so that made up for it—I wanted to see the world."

In December 1948 their son Eric arrived. Money was tight, so Helen took a job at Cannon Mills. "A lady at the trailer park watched him while I worked," she said.

James was offered a church in a tiny town in Idaho in 1952, so the fam-

JAMES AND HELEN LOER WITH SON ERIC, 1949.

ily made their first cross-country move, a move that proved difficult for Helen. "I was so homesick, I couldn't stand it," she said. "My three-year-old son said, 'Mama, I'll take you back to Grandma's in my wagon.'" And her father's words weighed heavily on her mind. "A year later we were offered a church in Sandpoint, Idaho, and I've never been homesick since."

It's a good thing, because although they eventually returned and retired to Idaho, there were many states and many churches in between. Helen smiled. "Our life has been really hectic!"

Financial struggles and frequent moves only served to draw them closer. "We've had to make lots of choices, but we've done them together," she said. "He was offered some good jobs, but he always chose the ministry." The former sailor pastored churches across the country, usually staying for four years before moving on.

In 1962 the couple welcomed a daughter, Candace (Kandi). Helen was thrilled. "I'd been wanting a girl so bad!" While James pastored, Helen took jobs with the federal government wherever they lived, usually working for the U.S. Forest Service.

Finally, in 2005, James officially retired from ministry. However, he didn't sit back in a rocking chair, and neither did Helen. The couple bought the historic Rathdrum Train Depot in 2009, and set about renovating the 1908 landmark. They currently use the building to host Bible studies on Sunday evenings.

James said, "We've really learned to know each other well enough." Then he laughed. "For instance, I know if I make a wrong choice I have to live with her and that wrong choice!"

That knowledge has served them both well. Helen smiled. "We love each other. Why fuss and fight?"

LOVE LESSON
"It's not one thing, but a combination of things that has held us together all these years. One thing that's been helpful is being a Christian, because you have spiritual help."— James Loer

---

JAMES AND HELEN LOER, 2010. *Photo courtesy Ralph Bartholdt*

CHAPTER 8
DAMN YANKEE

TEX SCOTT, 1942.　　　NICK GAYNOS, 1945.

Taking a Chance on Love — VERNON DUKE,
JOHN LA TOUCHE & TED FETTER, 1940

It took bravado, persistence and a $10 bet for a dashing Connecticut Yankee to win the heart of a petite Texas belle.

In the spring of 1943, Nick Gaynos and a friend were having drinks in the Bamboo Room of the Hotel Californian in Fresno. Both men were officers stationed nearby at Camp Pinedale. Long stalks of bamboo separated the bar from the dining room. Gaynos peered through the stalks and saw two young women having dinner. He called his friend over.

"I said, 'See that redhead? I'm going to marry her,'" Nick recalled. "My friend said, 'No way!' I said, 'I'll bet ya $10.'" And the wager was on. His friend seriously underestimated him, but he shouldn't have. The handsome lieutenant had already displayed the steely resolve and determination that would mark his military career. Nick had enlisted in the Army at age 23. "I wanted to fight Hitler," he said.

But he found himself facing a different enemy at Pearl Harbor on December 7, 1941. "I'd been up until 4 a.m. at my radio station," he recalled.

As a young private, he was in charge of air/ground communications at Hickam Air Field. He was asleep in his bunk when the earsplitting scream of airplane engines and the rat-a-tat sound of bullets strafing the barracks woke him. Grabbing his pants and his helmet, he scrambled out the door.

As he ran down the beach back toward his duty station, a Japanese Zero strafed the sand around him. Nick hit the ground and covered his head. He said he felt a hot breeze and heard a whistling sound inches from his ears. He looked up and saw the face of the pilot as he flew alongside him. The pilot grinned. When he got up he discovered a large piece of shrapnel next to him. "I grabbed it," he said. "It was still hot from the explosion."

After Pearl Harbor he'd been sent to Officer Candidate School, and quickly moved up through the ranks. Now, he focused that same kind of drive on the red-haired girl across the dining room.

"He sent the waiter over three times, offering to buy us drinks," Tex recalled, shaking her head. "We already had Cokes." She sent the waiter away. The 20-year-old southern belle had moved to Fresno and was living with her aunt because her parents thought she'd have better job opportunities in California than in Texas.

After the waiter returned for the third time without a drink order, Nick took matters into his own hands and approached the table. Tex wasn't sure what to make of the young officer. "I thought 'damn Yankee' was one word, until I met Nick," she said, with a smile. Finally, she agreed to let him buy her a soft drink. "You drink Coke?" he asked. She nodded.

"With what?" he pressed.

Tex raised an eyebrow. "With ice," she replied.

She laughed as she recalled that first meeting. "I guess he thought I'd be a cheap date!"

Before Nick left that night, he had her phone number. He called the next day and wanted to meet her aunt, so Tex agreed. "My aunt said she liked him better than any of the other fellows who'd been hanging around," said Tex. But the fiery redhead wasn't so sure.

"I wasn't wasting any time. I had a $10 bet on the line. I knew I needed to move fast," said Nick.

When he discovered that hamburgers were her favorite food, he took her to Fink's, a local eatery famous for their burgers.

"I had the best hamburger I'd ever tasted," Tex said with a sigh.

Nick felt pretty confident that he'd won her heart after that delicious meal. "I figured I had it locked in and my $10 was safe." So when Tex told him she'd gotten engaged to another suitor, it came as quite a shock. "I didn't take that real well," Nick admitted. But he also didn't let it deter him from his pursuit.

When he found out that Tex and her friends were having lunch at a local hotel with a large swimming pool, Nick took action. "I put on my bathing suit," he said. "The restaurant faced the pool so I flexed my abs and did my dives." Alas, Tex was unimpressed. "She never did come out," he said.

"I thought he was silly," she said. But later that day, friends told her Nick's performance had resulted in a nasty sunburn, which earned him some sympathy. Tex agreed to dinner—hamburgers, of course. After that

NICK AND TEX GAYNOS
WEDDING, JULY 3, 1943.

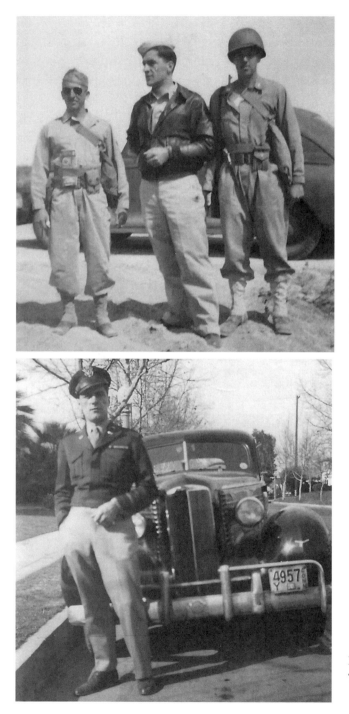

NICK GAYNOS
(CENTER),
CALIFORNIA,
1944.

NICK GAYNOS,
TEXAS, 1944.

date, she returned her suitor's engagement ring, and accepted Nick's proposal. Six weeks later on July 3, 1943, they were married in her Aunt Ruby's home. "I don't believe in long engagements," Nick said. As he walked down the aisle, his friend held out a $10 bill, and Nick scooped it up. "I never miss a bet."

That was almost 70 years ago and the sassy Texan and the handsome Yankee have travelled the world together. He saw the beginning of World War II and he saw the ending when he served as a key communications correspondent for General Douglas MacArthur.

A son, Scott, was born in 1946 and when he was three, he boarded a ship with his mother and traveled to Tokyo where Nick was stationed. While in Japan, daughter Nikki completed the family.

Nick served over 23 years in the military, achieving the rank of colonel, and they moved 20 times during those years. The large piece of shrapnel from Pearl Harbor came with them to every post. Tex truly enjoyed the travel, remembering that as a little girl, "I always wanted to see what was going on someplace else." The couple endured long separations, but Tex took it all in stride. "She was a great service wife," Nick said, proudly.

"I took care of myself and our two children," she explained. "When Nick was away, I always talked to the kids about their dad. I never felt sorry for myself. Caring for my family was a joy." But scrapbooks show she did much more than that. As the president of the Officers' Wives Club, she staged fashion shows, hat contests and flower shows. "His boss asked me to take care of the officers' wives and keep them happy, so I did," said Tex. "That was my job."

When Nick retired from the military in 1963, the couple both enjoyed thriving real estate careers in California.

Laughter punctuated their conversation as they talked about their life together. Nick produced a scrapbook and pointed to a telegram he'd sent Tex in 1968. It read, "Dear Tex, It took a long time but I finally got a good looking Greek, too. Jackie." As they chuckled together over Nick's telegram, he said, "I always think a sense of humor is vital to a marriage."

And that shared good humor has produced 70 years of happiness. Tex grinned at her husband. "We have had a lot of fun."

LOVE LESSON

"A good attitude is the secret to a happy relationship. Accept the person you married and don't constantly find fault."—Tex Gaynos

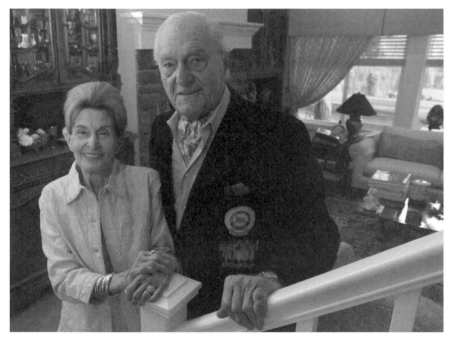

NICK AND TEX GAYNOS, 2010. *Photo courtesy Ralph Bartholdt*

Tex Gaynos died June 3, 2014.

CHAPTER 9
GLOBE TROTTERS

BILL AND JAY WARREN, WEDDING, AUGUST 20, 1949.

🌿 *Let's Get Away From it All—* MATT DENNIS & TOM ADAIR, 1941

Drafted into the Army in 1944 at age 18, Bill Warren served his country for two years—most of it in the European theater. The experiences he endured at such a tender age profoundly affected him. "I shipped out to Europe," he recalled. "We were replacement troops for those lost in the Battle of the Bulge. We were a task force trained for fighting." The young soldier was part of an ammunition and pioneer platoon engaged in a fierce struggle along the Siegfried line. "Our goal was Saarbrucken," he explained, describing the city situated near the French border.

"Because we were a munitions group, we were sent out at night," he said.

One night he fell into an exhausted sleep under a table. "They were looking for me to go out on patrol, but they couldn't find me." He paused and glanced down at his hands. "Out of the 12 men who went out that night,

61

only one came back." He doesn't gloss over his combat experience. "A lot of it was horrible—nothing to glorify war." Like many soldiers, he returned home wondering why he'd been spared when so many others were not. All he knew was that he wanted to live a life that mattered.

BILL WARREN, 1945.

Part of living that life began with a blind date in 1946, in Troy, New York.

Upon his discharge from the Army, Bill had enrolled at Rensselaer Polytechnic Institute in New York. A fraternity buddy set him up with Elizabeth "Jay" Lee, who was attending college nearby. They went to a football game, followed by supper and dancing at the fraternity house.

"Honestly, I remember thinking, I wasn't impressed with Bill," Jay recalled. Instead she viewed the date as a way to meet other fellows in his fraternity. Bill, however, was smitten and immediately wanted to ask for another date. Unfortunately, he couldn't remember Jay's last name. "But my friend told me, so I gave her a call."

By 1947 they were an item. "We met each other's families," Jay said. "And our mothers had tea one afternoon." Long conversations about world affairs, travel and children became a hallmark of their courtship. "I've always enjoyed being with her," said Bill. They both wanted children and were keenly interested in exploring the world around them, but when it came to politics, the discussions were a bit more heated.

Jay laughed and said, "Let me put it this way, we talked politics—eventually we agreed. My dad was a strong Democrat and Bill's dad was a Republican."

During the summer of 1948, they found jobs in Cape Cod at an inn. "There was a lake across the street, and a mountain with a lookout tower,"

Jay said. One evening, they hiked up to the lookout tower, and Bill took a ring out of his pocket and proposed. Jay's parents were staying in a nearby motel, and the excited couple pounded on their door and woke them, to share the news.

"My dad said, 'We have to toast this!'" said Jay. "But all they had in the motel room was scotch and cranberry juice, so that's what we toasted our engagement with."

They married on August 20, 1949, in Highland Falls, New York, and a year later moved to Colorado so Bill could pursue a master's degree in management engineering. He thought he'd left military service behind him, but halfway through the year, he was recalled by the Army. The Korean War had begun, and because he'd done ROTC in college, this time Bill went in as a 2nd lieutenant. "I served a year and a half and never had to go overseas," he said.

In 1951, the couple moved to Texas where Bill taught school and the first of their children arrived. When they'd

BILL AND JAY, DATING, 1948.

been dating, the couple had talked about how many children they wanted. They agreed four kids would be nice, but six would be perfect. They ended up with seven. Jay said large families were common at the time. "I think it was a result of having lived through the war years," she said. "It was a relief. The world was positive—at least our little part of it was."

Bill received his master's degree in 1954 and accepted a job at Harvard Business School. A succession of teaching jobs took the growing family across the east coast. Eventually, they wound up in Massachusetts where Bill worked in the education department of Polaroid. While there they heard about President Kennedy's Peace Corps. "In those long talks we had before we married, we talked about wanting to work overseas," Jay said.

When Bill was offered a position with the newly formed Peace Corps he immediately took it, without discussing it with his wife. He knew she'd be thrilled—and she was. "It was like something wonderful dropped in our laps," she said. So with six kids under ten, they moved to the Philippines.

"Our families were wonderfully supportive," Jay said. "They never once said, What the hell are you guys doing!?" After two years in the Philippines, the family traveled to Nepal, where Bill served as Peace Corps Director for a year.

In 1964 they moved to New Jersey, where their seventh child was born. They weren't there long—Bill had taken a job with the Education Development Center and was soon asked if he'd be willing to relocate to Kenya, so once again, the family eagerly embarked on a new adventure. Bill enjoyed his work. "I developed hands-on science material for kids in English-speaking areas of Africa," he said. "That program is still being used in eight countries." Jay found plenty to do as well. "She was never home," Bill said, laughing. Thanks to household help, she was able to work in local orphanages and implement adoption programs.

From Kenya, they returned to the States. Bill took a job as an elementary school principal in Massachusetts, and when their youngest child started kindergarten, Jay went back to college, eventually earning a master's degree in social work. She worked for an educational collaborative, and after 14 years as a school principal, Bill joined her, taking a position as a therapist for troubled teens.

In the late 1980s they both began to cut back their caseloads, and finally retired in 1992. Several years ago Bill was diagnosed with Parkinson's disease and once again they decided to move cross-country—this time to be near their two youngest children.

When asked the secret to a six-decade marriage, Jay shook her head and laughed. "I don't give advice anymore." Bill said choosing the right person is paramount. "Marrying Jay was the best decision I ever made," he said. "She's the most wonderful person in the world. I have Parkinson's but she is there for me. My nickname for her is Wonder Woman."

His wife shrugged off his praise. "I don't do anything major—I button his buttons," she said.

"Driving is major!" Bill countered.

"Yes, I do the driving now," she agreed. Then she smiled at him. "He's just my Bill."

From their living room they turned their gaze to a picture window and watched as a storm swept in. Bill cleared his throat. "Wherever we traveled, as long as we were together—it was home."

LOVE LESSON

"When went through difficult patches, we sought therapy. No shame in that. It's a good thing to know when to ask for help."—Jay Warren

---

BILL AND JAY WARREN, 2011. *Courtesy Colin Mulvany,* Spokesman Review

Bill Warren died April 14, 2014

CHAPTER 10
LITTLE THINGS ADD UP TO LOVE

HARVEY SHAW, HAWAII, 1944.

🌿 *This Heart Of Mine* — HARRY WARREN & ARTHUR FREED, 1946

S he first saw him in the hallway at Central Valley High School, and
six decades later Bonnie Shaw's eyes sparkle at the memory. Harvey
Shaw, home on leave, had stopped by his old school to visit his
brother and sister. His Navy uniform drew her eyes and set him apart from
the throngs of teenage boys. But despite his uniform, Harvey was just a boy
himself. "I got stupid and quit school right in the middle of my sophomore
year," he recalled. "I just didn't think. A few months later, I was in the Navy."

He said he chose to serve in the Navy because he didn't want to "get
stuck in the Army." Plus, he said, "I loved to swim!"

Though they'd not been introduced, and Harvey would soon leave to
join the crew of the escort carrier USS *Kwajalein* in the Pacific, Bonnie didn't
forget about the handsome sailor. And that sailor had his hands full. "I was
a quartermaster and worked in navigation. I steered the ship and mapped
the charts," he said.

Harvey counts himself fortunate that he didn't see much action. By the time the escort carrier launched in May of 1944, he said, "The Japanese were already outmanned." Instead of the action he thought he'd see, "All I saw was miles of nothing but water and some wonderful sunsets." Most of their threats came from Mother Nature. "We were in a beauty of a typhoon. I was so scared!" But when the aircraft carrier lifted up into the waves, he held course and steered the ship into them. All that time aboard ship had the consequences one might expect. "All of us green sailors got seasick at one point or another."

While docked in Hawaii, he welcomed the opportunity to dig his toes into sandy beaches and pose for pictures beneath palm trees to send the folks back home. His shipboard uniform consisted of dungarees and white cotton t-shirts, but off ship he sported the white uniform and jaunty cap that Bonnie had found so appealing.

By the time he returned home in 1946, Bonnie had graduated and had a steady boyfriend. One night she and her date pulled into the service station where Harvey worked. Her date said, "Hey, I know that guy!" He then brought Harvey over to the car and introduced him to Bonnie. Harvey nodded and said hello, but that was all. "I remember feeling real bad that he ignored me because I was with somebody else," Bonnie said.

They frequently ran into each other while out and about with their respective dates. Harvey liked Bonnie from that first formal introduction, but she had a boyfriend. "And I didn't like that at all," he said. However, when a mutual friend told him that Bonnie and her boyfriend had broken up, he didn't waste much time. "Four days later, I gave her a call," he said with a grin.

HARVEY SHAW AT THE WHEEL OF THE USS *KWAJALEIN*, 1944.

HARVEY SHAW (HANDS ON HIPS) AND BUDDIES AT SEA, 1944.

They spent many hours of their courtship on the dance floor. Bonnie said, "We both loved ballroom dancing." They also shared a sadder bond, both having lost brothers in combat in Italy during the war.

Every minute they spent with each other made them long for more. "I had liked him without ever really admitting it to myself and I think he felt the same way," said Bonnie. "When we finally got together, we just really fell in love."

Bonnie introduced him to her family. "My folks always said they didn't care who I married as long as he was Irish and Catholic." Well, Harvey was half-Irish, and when he knew he wanted to marry Bonnie he began taking instruction from Father Reilly at St. John Vianney. However, he didn't breathe a word of this to his sweetheart.

Bonnie grew worried when her friends peppered her with stories of an impending proposal. She loved Harvey, but she wasn't about to marry outside her faith. So, unbeknownst to Harvey, Bonnie paid a visit to Father Reilly, who informed her that Harvey was taking instruction. "He got the biggest kick out it when I told him I didn't know," she recalled. But Bonnie was not amused. In fact, she said, "I was a little bit miffed!"

In addition, her friends seemed to know more about Harvey's feelings for her than she did. "They were all saying, 'Harvey's in love with you—he wants to marry you!' I said well, why hasn't he told me?" Frustrated, she repeated the conversations she'd had with Father Reilly and her friends to Harvey. The result? He promptly proposed. He gave her an engagement ring under the clock at a local airfield. He'd used the GI Bill to take flight lessons and had earned his private pilot's license. On August 19, 1950, the couple married at the church where Harvey had been taking instruction. Sixty-four years later, they still attend that church.

While his marital plans were successful, his flight plans were not. He'd hoped to earn a commercial pilot's license, but that goal was derailed. "I got stupid one day and started buzzing all my buddies' houses—right over the rooftops." He shrugged. "The State Patrol told the owner what I was doing with his airplane and that was the end of the commercial license," he said.

Instead, he pursued a career in another form of transportation, and got a job with United Trucklines. Then, in 1958 he went to work for Colliers Motors, and worked there until he retired 32 years later.

Before they married they'd talked about how many children they'd like to have. "We wanted a dozen," said Bonnie, laughing. "But we settled for six." Even with a houseful of children, the couple still danced. "We both loved the waltz," said Harvey. "There are so many variations. We treasured that time."

Bonnie smiled at him. "He's such a good dancer!"

BONNIE AND HARVEY SHAW
WEDDING, AUGUST 19, 1950.

After retirement the pair traveled extensively. Harvey attended 12 reunions of the USS *Kwajalein*. "We pretty much covered the United States," said Bonnie "Harvey is such a history buff. He always found wonderful places for us to see and made it really exciting."

Both say their 6 children, 17 grandchildren and 8 great-grandchildren are precious to them and credit their shared faith for their lasting union. But it's the little things that make their love so special. Bonnie gives Harvey a nightly back rub and the last words they whisper before falling asleep are 'I love you.'

"He spoils me rotten," Bonnie said. "When I get up in the morning, my coffee and the paper are waiting for me."

Her eyes filled as she smiled at him. "Harvey is my heart."

LOVE LESSON

"I don't understand why so many couples spend so much time apart and go their separate ways. We've always preferred to be together."—Bonnie Shaw

---

HARVEY AND BONNIE SHAW, 2010.

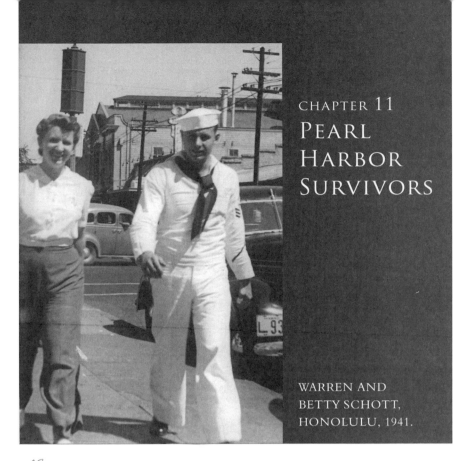

CHAPTER 11
PEARL
HARBOR
SURVIVORS

WARREN AND
BETTY SCHOTT,
HONOLULU, 1941.

I Don't Want to Walk Without You
—JULES STYNE & FRANK LOESSER, 1941

W arren Schott was a 20-year-old sailor when a friend offered to set him up with the new girl in town. "Don't do me any favors," Warren replied. He wasn't looking for love. But on the Fourth of July 1935, love found him anyway.

Warren had enlisted in the U.S. Navy earlier that year, during the height of the Great Depression, and he was in no hurry to settle down. He had plans to see the world. Besides, at the time he was earning just $21 a month. Still, he agreed to his friend's plan—after all, it was Independence Day and he figured one date does not a commitment make.

Betty Forest had just moved to Los Angeles. Her date with Warren was the day after she got to town. New girl indeed! "I liked him," she said with a smile. "He was fun."

That one date became lost in a blur of other dates over the next two years. Because their mutual friends were dating, Warren and Betty spent a lot of time together. Eventually, Warren decided they might as well spend the rest of their lives together. Neither of them can quite recall the details of Warren's proposal, but he is clear on one thing. "It wasn't any bended-knee affair," he said, chuckling.

While his proposal may have lacked romance, whatever he said proved enough to persuade Betty to become his bride. They were married April 2, 1938 at the Wee Kirk O' the Heather Chapel at Forest Lawn Cemetery in Los Angeles. Betty wore a dress her mother had made, which was crafted so beautifully that Betty didn't realize until after the wedding that she'd been wearing the dress inside out! She was the only girl in the office where she worked, and was touched when the guys pitched in and bought her a wedding bouquet of pink roses.

BETTY SCHOTT WEDDING
PORTRAIT, APRIL 2, 1938.

WARREN SCHOTT'S
MILITARY ID.

Betty laughed and said, "We got married in a cemetery and honeymooned in Death Valley, so we got all that out of the way!"

They had barely adjusted to married life when the Navy ordered Warren to Ford Island, Hawaii, the Naval Air Station inside Pearl Harbor. At the time, he was a first class petty officer in charge of small boat repair. Betty had to stay behind and earn her own money for passage, but she was determined to join her husband. In August 1939 she arrived on tiny Ford Island.

"We had quarters just up from Battleship Row," Warren recalled. "Our bedroom overlooked the runway."

The couple was used to noise, but the sounds that woke them on Dec. 7, 1941, were unlike anything they'd heard before. Betty pulled on her robe and looked out the bathroom window.

"Warren!" she called, "there's smoke and fire at the end of the runway."

At first he didn't believe her. But at his wife's insistence, he went to another window and spotted a plane flying low overhead. "I saw the red balls on the wings of the plane," he said. "I watched that plane torpedo the USS *Utah*. I said, 'Betty, we're at war!'"
They hustled out of their quarters and stopped to pick up a young mother and her two kids who lived downstairs. "It was total chaos," said Warren of the surprise attack. "We didn't know what to do." The horrific noise of the bombs, planes and machine-gun fire added to the overwhelming terror. Warren gathered everyone in the neighbor's car and took off for the administration building. "Barbara and I were in our nightgowns and robes, and shrapnel was falling from the sky," Betty said.

"The road was shredded by machine-gun fire," Warren said, as he recalled their frightening journey. Steering the vehicle away from the strafing fire of a Japanese warplane, he found shelter in a supply building. There Betty, her friend and the children, waited out the first wave of the attack. "They put us to work immediately," Betty said. "We unloaded guns and filled fire extinguishers."

Later, she and other Navy families found

WARREN AND BETTY
AT THE ALOHA TOWER,
JULY 1941.

shelter in the bachelor officers' barracks. They assumed the attack would be followed by a Japanese invasion of the island, but the invasion never came. "It was just chaotic," Betty said, "so many injuries and dead in the water."

Warren returned to his duty station. "We were at war, and none of us had any experience," he said. "I took one of boats and picked up our fellows who were in the water along Battleship Row." The men he pulled out of the harbor were covered in oil. Afterward, Betty discovered, "They got rid of every towel in my house trying to help clean them up. Finally they took down my kitchen curtains and used them." Over the years they've talked about everything, but on one topic Warren remained silent. "He never talked about the people he pulled out of the oily water that morning," Betty said. "Never."

At 8:00 that night, Warren found Betty and brought her some clothes, since she'd worn her pajamas and bathrobe all day. When she returned home, she couldn't find their kitten anywhere and feared the worst. Ten days later, Betty found her huddling in a small section of their stove.

Communication had been cut off to the mainland, so their families had no idea if they'd survived—Betty's mother even wrote to President Roosevelt. Finally, a telegram arrived, relieving the minds of the worried parents back home.

Soon after the attack, the military began evacuating women and children, but Betty refused to leave. For the next year she steadfastly ignored the pleading of officials and stayed with Warren. Finally, in May 1942 they were transferred stateside. Ironically, Betty realized they'd ended up on the same ship, but since Warren was on duty, she had no way to tell him. To his delight, as he walked up the gangplank he spotted his wife waving at him from the ship's rail. "We were practically the last people to move off Ford Island," Betty said. They'd both survived the horror of the 'day that will live in infamy,' but time can't erase the memories of the tragedy they watched unfold.

They traveled to Norfolk, VA where Warren attended a diesel engine program. On Dec. 6, 1942, the Schotts welcomed their first child, Warren Jr. (Skip). What better way to honor the lives of those lost than to celebrate a new life? The celebration was short-lived however; Warren was soon shipped off to Australia and Okinawa. Betty had moved to Cleveland to stay with his parents and Warren got to see his son briefly, when Skip was 10 days old. Two years would pass before he'd see him again, the first of several such extended separations. Betty shrugged off the hardship. "You just do what you have to do," she said.

In January 1946, after 12 years in the Navy, Warren was honorably discharged. The family settled in Washington state and another son, Robert John (Bobby) arrived in November of 1946. And in 1949, Warren built the home they would share for 65 years. "We got the plans from Better Homes and Gardens magazine," Betty said. The fact that Warren had never built a home before didn't daunt him.

WARREN SCHOTT, 1945.

"Give him a challenge, and he can do it," Betty said.

"I built every stick of it myself," Warren said, as he looked with pride on the home he'd created for his family.

Warren worked for the Corp of Engineers, the Atlas Missile program and the General Services Administration (GSA) until he retired in 1973, at the age of 55. The Schotts recently celebrated their 75th anniversary and attribute the longevity of their marriage to friendship. A plaque hanging in their kitchen says, "Happiness is being married to your best friend."

Betty said, "We just get along. We finish each others' sentences."

Her husband flashed a grin and deadpanned, "She's put up with me all these years and she hasn't hit me yet."

As Pearl Harbor survivors, Betty acknowledges that fate has smiled kindly on them. "A lot has gone on in our lives, but we just seem to come out on the right side of it," she said. "We've been incredibly lucky."

LOVE LESSON

"Everything's built on friendship. He's been my best friend for 77 years."
—Betty Schott

WARREN AND BETTY SCHOTT, 2010. *Photo courtesy Ralph Bartholdt*

Warren died May 19, 2014

CHAPTER 12
BROTHERS AND THEIR BRIDES

GENE AND EVIE FELS, 1944.

🌿 *The Boy Next Door* — HUGH MARTIN & RALPH BLANE, 1944

A festive feeling permeated Gene and Evie Fels home. Gene's brother Wilbert (Joe) and his wife, Nora, had stopped by to discuss the secrets to a happy marriage. "We have a party going on!" Nora said.

It would be hard to find couples with better qualifications to talk about enduring relationships—long marriages run in the Fels family. In November 2009, Gene and Evie celebrated their 64th wedding anniversary, and Joe and Nora had celebrated their 64th anniversary in May. That's 128 years of marital experience.

Indeed, the Felses have much to celebrate. Gene and Joe, both World War II veterans, grew up in a large family in the Chelan, Washington area. Both men vividly recall the first time they met their brides. "There was this new girl in town who worked at the café. The fellas said she wouldn't go out with anyone—no one could date her," said Gene. But instead of backing away from the challenge, Gene checked out the situation and the elusive Evie. He promptly bet his friends $5 that he could get a date with the beautiful waitress.

NORA FELS, HIGH SCHOOL
GRADUATION PHOTO

Evie sighed and said, "I don't remember how many times he asked me out."

Gene admitted his persistence might have been tinged with desperation. "I had to get her to go out with me," he said. "I didn't have $5 to pay the bet!"

When Evie finally relented, the two quickly became inseparable. "I must have impressed her," Gene asserted. "I've kept her 64 years."

However, World War II intruded into the couple's blossoming romance. "My dad said he'd give me $50 if I didn't get married before I went overseas," said Gene. He accepted his father's offer, but six decades later he shook his head and said, "I never did get that 50 bucks!"

When asked which branch of the service he joined, Gene replied, "I didn't join nothing! They took me in 1943." As an 18-year-old high school student, he received a three-month deferment so he could graduate, and

WILBERT AND NORA FELS (ON LEFT) WITH FRIENDS, 1944.

afterwards was sent to Army boot camp. From there it was on to North Africa for two weeks, and then straight into combat in Italy.

Joe and Nora's romance also began in an unconventional manner. "I pushed her into the lake," said Joe. His excuse? He simply couldn't resist the temptation. "Well, she kept standing right in front of me," he explained. Nora reached over and gave him playful pat. "I was having my swimming lessons," she said. Fortunately, she'd learned enough to stay afloat after her abrupt introduction to Joe.

He certainly got her attention, and she began walking her dog past the Fels' home

GENE FELS, 1943.

almost every day. Joe and his brothers would whistle appreciatively as she strode by and soon enough she and Joe were a couple.

When Joe received his draft notice, he wasn't allowed to finish high school like his older brother. Instead, he had to report immediately to Far-

GENE FELS, ITALY, 1945.

ragut Naval Training Center and from there was sent to San Pedro, California. Having seen Gene and Evie separated by war, he was determined to marry Nora before he shipped out.

He secured a 72-hour pass and told Nora to make wedding plans. However, in the excitement of his leave and upcoming nuptials, he lost his wallet. He called his intended from San Pedro and she wired him money for a plane ticket. Joe arrived in Seattle and caught a bus for Chelan. Once again, bad luck intervened. The bus got caught in a freak spring snowstorm. "I called my brother, Wes," Joe said. "He came and got me."

Joe and Nora married on May 14, 1945. After a one-day honeymoon, he had to return to base and then he shipped out to the Pacific. "I was fortunate," he said. "I went through 11 major engagements and never got a scratch."

Gene wasn't so lucky. He reached into a cabinet in the corner of his living room and drew out a small box. Wiping the dust off it, he opened it to reveal the Purple Heart medal nestled within. "I got blowed out of my foxhole," he said with a shrug. "A mortar shell threw me 30 feet into a rock pile. I broke my jaw." He grew quiet. "Half of my company was lost on that hill in Italy that day." After a month-long hospital stay, Gene returned to the battlefield.

Evie's letters were his lifeline to a world he hoped he'd see again. "I wrote to him most every day," she said. Gene recalled a Valentine from Evie he opened in a foxhole. He'd unfolded the large card, grabbed a pen and filled the backside with a long letter to his love. "I didn't want to waste the space!" She didn't know what to think when the card she'd sent her sweetheart returned to her mailbox. Fortunately, she discovered his letter.

They married upon his discharge from the Army in November 1945.

After the war, both brothers began careers in the automotive repair industry. When Joe and Nora moved to Spokane Valley, Washington, Joe said, "I talked Gene into coming over here." He laughed. "Then we moved to Colville!" They raised their two daughters there, but eventually returned to Spokane Valley, settling less than a mile away from Gene and Evie.

And while laughter filled the room as the couples reminisced, things haven't always been easy for them. At age 70, Nora was diagnosed with Huntington's disease, a degenerative nervous system disorder. And Evie suffers from dementia.

The brothers are now caregivers for the women who spent so many years caring for them. "It's his turn to do the cooking," Nora said with a smile.

As the couples pondered the secrets to marital longevity, an answer occurred to Evie. While many memories have been lost to dementia, one thing is very clear to her. Reaching out she laid her hand on her husband's cheek. "He's a gem," she said.

Gene smiled. "She's been a good companion."

Joe guffawed at the growing sentimentality, but added that choosing your partner well is important. He grinned at Nora, "She's made life interesting." Growing serious he added, "If you communicate and work things out between you, there's nothing you can't solve." Silence descended after this statement, then Evie looked at Gene. "Maybe we'd better start doing that," she said with a grin.

Once again laughter filled the room. With 128 years of marriage between them, the Fels family, by anyone's standards, is doing just fine.

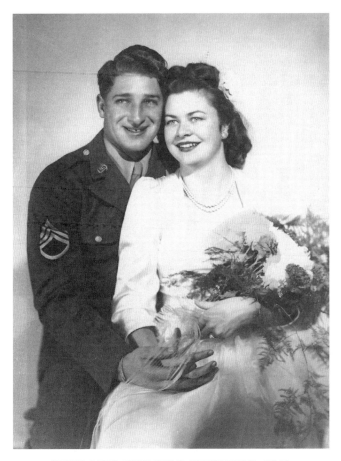

GENE AND EVIE FELS, WEDDING, 1945.

LOVE LESSON
"Every marriage has ups and downs, just be patient with each other."
—Wilbert (Joe) Fels

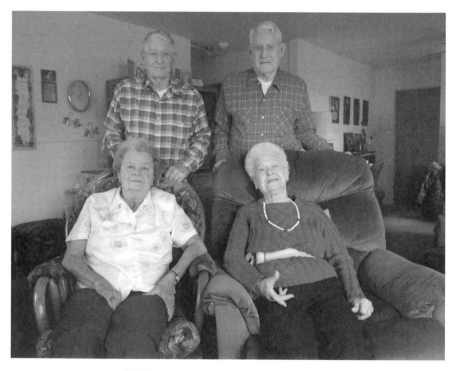

GENE, EVIE, JOE AND NORA, 2009.
Photo courtesy J. Bart Rayniak, Spokesman Review

Eugene Fels died February 18, 2010

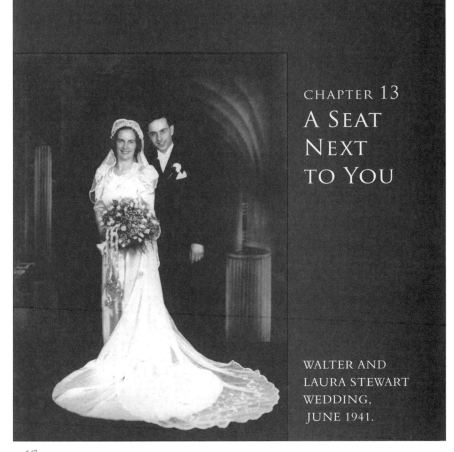

CHAPTER 13

A SEAT NEXT TO YOU

WALTER AND
LAURA STEWART
WEDDING,
JUNE 1941.

🌿 *Laura* — DAVID RASKIN & JOHNNY MERCER, 1945

A sophisticated Long Island gal met a boy from Detroit, in Indiana of all places, and launched a relationship that spanned seven decades—all thanks to a small slip of paper, drawn from a basket.

Walter Stewart and Laura Versfelt met at Fort Wayne Bible Institute in 1940. Each month, students drew scraps of paper with a table and seat number written on it to find out where they'd sit for meals in the dining room. "Lo and behold, after a few months, Walter was assigned to my table," recalled Laura. He made quite an impression. "He pulled my chair out for me. Most of the boys were farm boys, but Walter was from Detroit—he was a city boy," she said.

She'd had plenty of opportunities to observe the handsome young man. Walter led songs during their weekly services. "Each Friday night, he dressed up."

Walter found his feisty tablemate intriguing. "The other guys were scared of this girl from New York," he said. "So they dared me to ask her

83

out, and I did! We walked down to the park and back—a 45-minute date." But in those 45 minutes, he found a way to impress the city girl. "He knew the name of every bird we saw!" Laura said. While she didn't share his knowledge of ornithology, she was a singer and shared his passion for music.

"She was soloist, and music was a specialty of mine so we had something in common," Walter said. With a big concert approaching, he borrowed a car and asked Laura if she'd like to go with him. She agreed. Seventy years later, in their cozy living room, he stole a glance at her. "That was the first time you kissed me," he said.

"No! No! You rascal, you!" Laura said, laughing as she pushed at his shoulder.

Walter shrugged. Then he grinned and proceeded to tell the real story of their first kiss. "I kissed her in the hallway after a music lesson," he admitted. "I kissed her so hard you could hear it down the hall! SMACK!"

Though he said they were too poor to marry, he proposed anyway. When the school year drew to a close, she went home to Long Island and he traveled back to Detroit, but their separation didn't last long. "I bought a diamond ring for her and hitchhiked all the way to Long Island to give it to her. She was surprised to see me because she'd just written that it wouldn't be a good time to visit." He chuckled. "It's a good thing I left before that letter came!"

They both found employment in aircraft factories in Long Island, and when her mother realized Walter wasn't just another boyfriend, she gave her blessing and they plunged into wedding plans.

In June 1941, they married in Garden City Park on Long Island. Laura laughed when she recalled what transpired after the ceremony. "We sang together at the wedding reception and when we thought no one was looking, we snuck out through the kitchen and made our getaway."

But they weren't stealthy enough and soon found themselves followed by a caravan of cars. Walter's friends "kidnapped" him and treated him to ice cream before releasing him to his bride. Laura wasn't thrilled by the chain of events, but the experience later came in handy. "As a pastor's wife, I've told many a bride, whatever happens, just roll with it," she said.

They settled into married life and eagerly anticipated the birth of their first child, when tragedy struck. The baby died at birth. As Laura woke from the anesthesia, she said, "I heard a baby cry, then the doctor said, 'I'm sorry.'"

The loss was especially hard, as Walter had enlisted in the Navy and was soon to be shipped out. As he processed the loss of their child, he said, "I sat at the aircraft factory and cried like a baby. You plan for nine months and then it's just gone. It was a little girl." As he spoke, Laura looked at him, astonished. "You never told me that," she said. "You never told me you cried." He shrugged and looked away. The memory of that long-ago loss still hurts.

War doesn't wait for grief, and in December of 1943, Walter was sent to Hawaii and then on to Guam. "I didn't want to leave her—I was worried about her health." However, he found new concerns in the South Pacific. Walter has never forgotten the things he saw, though he often wishes he could. "Shot up, devastated, rotting corpses—the smell was horrible. It was like a horror movie when we got there."

Laura said, "I'll bet there are stories I never did hear."

Walter served two and half years. "That was enough for me," he said. "I couldn't wait to get home."

Laura was waiting for him. "I can still see him in that little white sailor hat," she recalled. No band played as he walked toward her, but

WALTER STEWART, HAWAII, 1944.

after being apart for two years, just the sight of him proved more exciting than a ticker tape parade. That isn't to say their reunion went smoothly. Like many couples separated by the war, the Stewarts had to readjust to life together. "It felt strange at first," she said. I'd gotten used to being on my own."

Laura had a good job that paid the bills and had her own way of doing things. She smiled, "He found out his wife had become a little independent." Walter took the changes in stride, but eventually said, "We need to talk this over!" And talk they did. Their deep love for each other and their shared faith helped ease the transition.

LAURA SPENDING CHRISTMAS WITHOUT WALTER, 1943.

The G.I. Bill enabled Walter to attend Gordon College in Boston. Sadly, as he pursued his ministerial degree, Laura lost another baby. This time it was a boy. "I carried him almost six months," she said. "After the second baby, I was through. I didn't want any children." And Walter? As he packed away the unused baby clothes in a cedar chest, he wept, dampening the tiny outfits with his tears. Shaking her head with the memory, Laura said, "I don't understand how couples break up at a time like that—we needed each other so."

Following graduation in 1948, they moved west and pastored churches in the Portland, Oregon area, where Walter enrolled in seminary. He hadn't given up his dream of being a father. "I broached the subject of having another baby," he said.

It didn't go well. "If I'd had a gun, I would have shot him," Laura said. She still felt raw from the loss of her first two babies. But one year after that conversation she gave birth to a daughter, Roberta Joy. Five years later at the age of 42, she found out she was expecting again. "I told the doctor, if I'm pregnant it's a miracle. The doctor replied, "Well, I found a miracle and it's a good-sized one!" Their daughter Laurie completed their family in 1959.

After raising their daughters and serving in many churches, the couple retired to Desert Hot Springs, California before eventually moving to the Pacific Northwest to be near their younger daughter.

The Stewarts credit their faith in God for their lasting marriage, and Laura's eyes still sparkle when she talks about her husband. "I knew in my heart that the love we had for one another was something you don't find in many marriages," she said. "Walter's always had a heart for his family and he's been the one to forgive and forget. I've been a tough egg to crack, but I've softened over the years."

And Walter is still thankful for that slip of paper that seated him at her table so long ago. His voice grew husky as he recounted their life together. He said, "She's what I needed to fill in the blanks."

LOVE LESSON
"A man who shows his emotions and is tender-hearted makes a good husband."—Laura Stewart

---

LAURA AND WALTER STEWART, 2010.

Walter Stewart died March 23, 2013

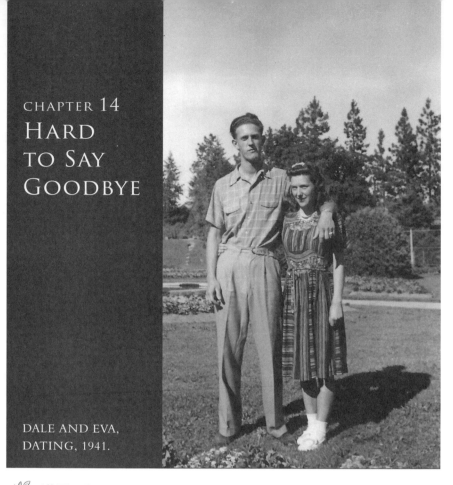

CHAPTER 14
HARD
TO SAY
GOODBYE

DALE AND EVA,
DATING, 1941.

🎵 *All Too Soon*—DUKE ELLINGTON & CARL SIGMAN, 1940

D
ale Eastburg has never forgotten the first time he saw his future
wife, Eva. Neither has she. "I was in the front yard and Dale
drove by on his motorcycle and nearly crashed, because he was
gawking at me," said Eva. "I almost hit a pole!" Dale confirmed. She was
used to being gawked at—her family had just moved to the area and Eva
was the only girl in a neighborhood filled with boys. It was 1939 and Dale,
a high school senior, asked one of the boys in the neighborhood to introduce
him the dark-haired beauty with the stunning smile. Soon they became inseparable.

Dale had three motorcycles. "The first one the fellas had to push him
up the street to start!" said Eva. But when it came time to take his girl out,
Dale borrowed a friend's car.

Eva attended a different school, but not for long. Dale grinned. "I talked
her into transferring to Rogers (his high school)." Reaching over and patting

his hand, Eva said, "He gave me the attention I probably needed. I had three brothers, but I was the only girl."

After graduation he enrolled at Gonzaga University. When his friends began receiving draft notices, Dale decided not to wait for his, and instead enlisted in the Army Air Corps.

"We knew we were going to get married," Eva said. "But when the war came along, that hurried things up." They no longer remember the details of the proposal, but Eva suspects Dale's mom had something to do with it. "His folks never had a girl—just two boys. They thought I was the daughter they never had and they didn't want to lose me." Her folks liked Dale, as well. Eva smiled. "He was handsome and very shy."

On May 5, 1942, the couple drove to a chapel in Idaho with both sets of parents and their minister and his wife. "We got married in a little white church—it's still there," Eva said. They didn't have much time to settle into married life, as Dale left for Fresno, California for basic training in March of 1943. But he missed his bride. Eva said, "He got so lonely, he called me and said, 'Quit your job and come to Fresno.'" So she left her job at Baxter hospital and traveled to California.

DALE EASTBURG, 1943.

From there she followed him to Texas and then to New Mexico where he completed his training. As part of the 12th Air Service Group, Dale knew he'd soon be shipping out for overseas duty. The thought of saying goodbye to his bride overwhelmed him. So, he didn't.

One morning Eva woke to an empty bed. She recalled, "We'd said our good-nights and went to sleep. He snuck out early the next morning while I slept." Tears fell as she clutched the pillow, still warm from his head. She didn't know when or if she'd see him again. Adding to the intensity of her sorrow was the fact that she was pregnant with their first child. More than two and a half years would pass before they saw each other again.

Dale traveled to China. "I belonged to the Flying Tigers," he said. "I worked on the airplanes during the day and was on a jeep with a machine gun at night." At one point, Dale said, the Japanese had the American base surrounded on three sides. "They never closed the gap. But they bombed us continually." He paused and shook his head. "It was not good. But we stopped the Japanese from coming. We bombed them every single day."

Eva wrote to him regularly. She still remembers the number she penned on every envelope: "19113108," she recites. But still, Dale said, "She really

DALE EASTBURG
(FAR RIGHT) AND
BUDDIES, CHINA
1944.

had no idea where I was." Life back in the States wasn't easy, either. Eva said, "Kids today don't know what war is about. Everything was rationed—shoes, gas, sugar!"

On February 18, 1944, she gave birth to a daughter, Diane. Though exhausted, she wrote to tell Dale. It took several months for him to get the news and when he did, there was still some confusion. He said, "Eva wrote a letter all about the baby. The baby this and the baby that! But she didn't mention the sex of the baby!" More letters ensued, including one that contained a picture of Eva and Diane, his blue-eyed daughter with curly golden hair.

Finally, in December 1945 Eva got a telegram. "COMING HOME" was all it said. Dale had served three years, three months and three days, and all he wanted was to come home to his wife and meet his daughter.

The week before Christmas a taxi pulled up in front of the house. "I stood back and waited and let his parents greet him," Eva said. "I'm a positive person, but his mother got sick with worry about him." After hugging his parents, Dale met his 22-month-old daughter. When he recalled that first glimpse of her, a grin split his face. "I couldn't believe it," he said, shaking his head. "You can't imagine."

Dale took a job with the W.P. Fuller Company as a commercial estima-

DALE (MIDDLE) AND
BUDDIES, CHINA 1944.

tor, and Eva had her hands full with their growing family. In 1948, daughter Linda arrived followed by Craig in 1954 and Cheryl in 1964.

Eva said her husband didn't want her to work outside the home, but he did make one exception. "The only time I went to work was to earn money to buy a boat!" she said, laughing. They needed one—the family lived for many years on the shores of a local lake.

Dale retired in 1987, but long before, he and Eva started a tradition— Friday night dates. Each Friday when he arrived home from work she'd be ready to go. They often went to a favorite place with a lovely city view and enjoyed a cocktail while watching the sunset. Then they'd choose a restau-

EVA AND DALE, 1945.   EVA AND DIANE.

rant for dinner. When they moved into town and away from the lake, they began another tradition—regular gym workouts. Dale, 92, and Eva, 90 are much loved members a local fitness facility. "We call them our family away from family," said Eva. Three times a week they hit the gym to walk and do strength training. "It keeps us happy and contented," she said.

And every Friday Dale wakes up and says, "Honey, this is our day to-day—don't forget our Friday engagement."

"As if I would!" Eva said with a grin. The only thing that's changed is now they go out to lunch instead of dinner.

Their close-knit family dotes on them. The Eastburgs have six grandsons and three great-granddaughters. And more than 70 years after they said "I do," their mutual affection is still evident. Dale says their secret to marital bliss is simple. "We love each other and we work together."

But the quiet man grew more eloquent as he gazed at his bride. "I appreciate everything about her," he said. "She couldn't be more perfect." Eva smiled, "Sometimes he tells me, 'Come here and sit down a minute.' When I ask him why, he says, 'Cause I just want to look at you.'"

LOVE LESSON

"Dale understands and forgives my shortcomings."—Eva Eastburg

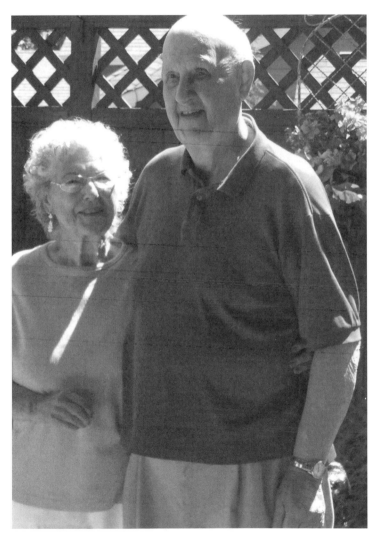

DALE AND EVA EASTBURG, 2012.

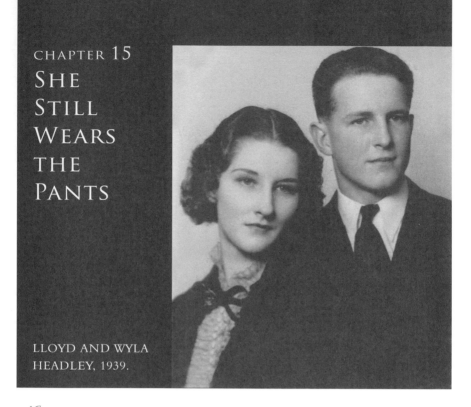

CHAPTER 15
SHE STILL WEARS THE PANTS

LLOYD AND WYLA
HEADLEY, 1939.

🌿 *Anything You Can Do* — IRVING BERLIN, 1946

L loyd Headley knows a good thing when he sees it. More than 70 years ago, at a Sunday school picnic, he glimpsed a pretty girl. While there were several attractive girls at the picnic that day, one stood out from the rest because of what she wore—white pants. "I saw her across the crick," he said. "In those days a girl wearing slacks was something!" Though only a freshman in high school, Lloyd made up his mind—Wyla was the one for him. "I knew she had everything I wanted." He grinned and added. "And I knew she'd wear the pants in the family."

He finagled his way into giving her a ride home from the picnic. And he eventually finagled his way into her heart. As winter sunlight seeped through the windows of their home, Wyla said after that picnic, "He never went with anybody else."

"See how I've suffered?" Lloyd retorted, shaking his head in mock despair. But he just didn't see any point in dating other girls when he already knew exactly who he wanted. A shared sense of humor is just one of the

94

things that has made this couple's marriage enduring. Wyla chuckled. "Yes, we've been married 70 years and we're still speaking—occasionally."

But the road to true love wasn't without a bump or two. "He wanted to get serious right away," she said. "But I was having fun. We never really went steady." Lloyd disagreed. He cleared his throat and explained, "I went steady—she didn't. She was dating everyone who asked!"

They saw each other on and off for five years. Wyla admitted Lloyd had grown on her, and the last two years before they married, she said, "We dated pretty steady." This was because Lloyd understood the value of persistence, and he also knew how to make a memorable impression. He drove by Wyla's house on the way to school each day, and one day he saw her brother waiting for the school bus and decided to stop and give him a ride. He slammed on the brakes and the car skidded on the loose gravel. "I flipped my dad's car," he recalled. "Right in front of her house." As the car settled on its side, the first face he saw through the window was Wyla's mother's. "I said, 'Oh no! They'll never let me go out with Wyla again.'" Fortunately, they allowed him to continue to see her, but from then on, Wyla's brother refused to ride with him.

After relentlessly pursuing his prize, on December 30, 1939, Lloyd and Wyla married. Or as Wyla said, "We came to a mutual agreement."

"I finally wore her down," said Lloyd. They chose that date because they both had a three-day holiday from work. Lloyd, 24, worked at Inland Chevrolet, and Wyla, 21, became a beautician. They bought a little house and in 1940, Wyla gave birth to a daughter. Their cozy domestic bliss was interrupted by the advent of World War II.

Wanting to do his part, Lloyd enlisted in the Air Force in 1942,

LLOYD HEADLEY, 1942.

hoping to become a pilot. However, he said, "I washed out of pilot school and ended up being an airplane mechanic. I worked on B-17's and later B-26s." At the ripe old age of 27, he didn't have a lot in common with many of the guys. "They called me Dad," he said. "Everybody else was 17, 18 and 19!"

His initial disappointment about not being able to fly waned when he discovered his assignments were all stateside, allowing Wyla and their daughter to join him. Even so, he wasn't disappointed when his enlistment ended. "I served three years and three months and couldn't get out soon enough," he said. In 1945, they made it home in time for Christmas.

Their family grew with the addition of two sons, and busy years followed. Like most couples they had their share of disagreements, and one in particular stands out. The issue that sparked the argument?

Plants.

According to Lloyd, his wife's green thumb had gotten out of control. "I love plants," Wyla admitted. One day he teased her once too often about the plants hanging in the kitchen, and his ribbing didn't go over well. Chuckling, he recalled, "She grabbed plants and started throwing them out in the yard. She threw them everywhere!" Later, she went out and salvaged what she could. Perhaps that's one reason Lloyd said the secret to a happy marriage is to "never hold a grudge. If you get mad, get over it as soon as possible."

While they may not share a love of plants, the couple found mutual pleasure in the lake cabin they purchased in 1965. The cabin became a focal point for fun and memories. Scrapbooks and albums filled with pictures document summer barbecues and family gatherings. "We have a big grill down on the beach and fixed the most delicious pancakes," Lloyd said. Each year the couple hosted an open house on the Fourth of July, taking pleasure in watching new generations create their own memories. "We thoroughly enjoyed it as parents," Wyla said. "Our kids enjoyed it when they came along and now our grandkids and great-grandkids are enjoying it."

In addition to time at the lake, the couple loves dancing, playing cards and bowling. "I didn't start bowling until I was 85," Lloyd said. Due to macular degeneration, Wyla is legally blind, so she has to trust her husband's direction when it's time to pick up a spare. "If I don't do well, it's all Lloyd's fault," she said. According to Lloyd, she needn't worry. "I've been blessed with good eyes and good reflexes," he said. But he does wish she wouldn't beat him so often.

Lloyd's dogged pursuit of the girl he first saw at a long-ago picnic has paid off in a lifetime of happiness. "It's been wonderful," Wyla said. "I would do it over again."

LOVE LESSON
"Sometimes I wanted to kill him, but never divorce him."—Wyla Headley

---

LLOYD AND WYLA HEADLEY, 2010. *Photo courtesy Ralph Bartholdt*

Wyla Headley died June 18, 2011
Lloyd Headley died November 5, 2011

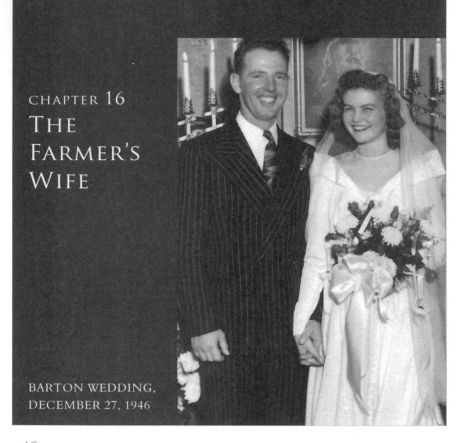

CHAPTER 16

THE
FARMER'S
WIFE

BARTON WEDDING,
DECEMBER 27, 1946

🌿 *Ain't Nobody Here But Us Chickens*
— ALEX KRAMER & JOAN WHITNEY, 1946

L ike many young women, Melba Jeanne Yates fantasized about the man she'd one day marry. He'd be handsome of course, and a Christian, but one thing he would *not* be was a farmer. Her ideas about the life of a farmer's wife made her shudder. "Feeding chickens and milking cows——none of that stuff appealed to me," she said.

But a blind date with Don Barton in December of 1945 changed everything. Don had just gotten out of the service and returned to the family farm on Half Moon Prairie. His brother played the saxophone in a local band and was dating Melba Jeanne's cousin. Her cousin wanted Melba Jeanne to attend a Grange dance with them, but her mother insisted Melba Jeanne had to be home by midnight. The problem? Grange dances didn't end until 1 AM.

Don's brother gave him a call and said, "We'll bring her, if you take her home." So Don agreed, and when he got to the Grange, Melba Jeanne was on the dance floor. "Somebody pointed her out to me," he recalled. "She looked like a cute little bobby socks girl!" The fact that she was dancing at all was something of a miracle. "I grew up in a family where dancing wasn't allowed," said Melba Jeanne. "My younger brother and I finally talked our parents into letting us learn how. They didn't know we were already practicing in the study hall at school during the noon hour!"

However, it wasn't her skills on the dance floor that won Don's heart. "She wasn't a very good dancer at that time," he said with a grin. But during the long drive from the Grange to her home, the two got better acquainted.

The attack on Pearl Harbor had prompted Don, 21, to drop out of college and enlist in the Air Force in 1942. His eyes lit up when he recalled the 60 hours he'd spent training in a Stearman biplane. "It was a fun airplane!" He was less enthusiastic about another training aircraft, the BT-13. "It was a two-seater with a canopy," he recalled. "I didn't care for it. About eight percent of our class was killed in the stupid plane during training." Don said that when the pilots initiated 1-1/2 spirals, often the plane tightened up and they were unable to pull out of the spiral. "I didn't take any chances," he said.

After earning his wings in 1943, he flew B-24s and was sent to instructor pilot school. He spent over a year training new pilots. "It was a good job," he said. But, he added, as the war went on and the need for pilots intensified, "They were scraping the bottom of the barrel. I got some real jugheads."

While he enjoyed flying and teaching, what he wanted more than anything was to experience combat. "I felt like I was being cheated," he said. "I didn't know the good Lord had his hand on my shoulder." When the military launched the B-29 program, Don volunteered, and spent five

DON BARTON, JULY 1943.

months learning to fly the aircraft. Since it was a new plane, it didn't have all the kinks worked out. Don experienced 13 engine failures during his 80 hours of training.

Finally he was assigned a crew, and in March of 1945 they flew to Guam. He had some close calls during his 25 missions over the Pacific, but one in particular he will never forget. "We made it to our target, but then got hit by a fighter. We got shot up pretty bad," he said. "I lost my navigator. He sat right behind me. He was the youngest one on the crew."

The memory haunts him. Don's eyes filled and his voice broke. "He was a nice kid—a real nice kid." While his crew grappled with the death of the young navigator, Don grappled with a plane that was falling apart. They couldn't land on Iwo Jima because it was socked in with fog, so the crew jettisoned everything they could as the plane sputtered and shook.

Don said, "I suggested we bail out over Iwo Jima, but the boys put up a fuss." They didn't want to abandon the body of their friend. He decided to try to land on Tinian, and did so with only two engines functioning and virtually no fuel. Don shook his head. "We shouldn't have made it."

He'd had his taste of combat and all he could think about was getting home to the farm. His final mission was flying over the USS *Missouri* as a show of force, while the Japanese formally tendered their surrender.

Two months after receiving his separation papers, he met Melba Jeanne, who was immediately smitten with her dance partner. After that initial date, Don put a lot of miles on his truck driving from his family farm to her home. When they couldn't see each other, they spoke on the phone. "At night I'd sit in the stairway and talk for hours to Don until someone on the party line would break in and want to make a call," Melba Jeanne said.

Soon they announced their engagement. "It didn't bother me that she said she'd never marry a farmer," said Don. Then he chuckled and looked across the room at his bride. "Love is blind." Even so, Melba Jeanne admitted, "I had to do a lot of thinking—even after we were engaged." But Don's patient persistence won her hand and her heart.

Their wedding on December 27, 1946 was tinged with sadness. Don's brother had been killed in a logging accident five days earlier. "My folks insisted we go ahead with the wedding. They said Jack would have wanted it." Don sighed. "He would have been my best man."

After a Canadian honeymoon, the coupled settled into married life. Don had promised his bride that she'd never have to do those farm chores she'd worried about, and he was true to his word. "No feeding chickens. No milking cows," she said, smiling.

In 1948, they welcomed their first daughter. Two years later, a second daughter joined them following a difficult birth—her identical twin was stillborn—and within a few months they knew something was wrong with the new baby. Melba Jeanne folded her hands and looked down. "We couldn't get the doctor to tell us." Finally they were told their daughter, Beverly, had cerebral palsy and the doctor advised them to place her in an institution. Don said, "They told us she can't hear, she'll never talk and she won't be able to see. We knew they were wrong." Beverly lived with them at home until she was 43 and is now happily living in a group home. "She has fantastic hearing," Melba Jeanne added.

A third daughter completed their family in 1952 and they raised their girls on the family farm. While Melba Jeanne didn't do farm chores, she certainly did her share of work, especially during harvest. "Her biggest job was cooking for the crews," Don said. "One year she cooked for 22 men!" She also drove truck during harvest. "Not because I had to. I enjoyed it!"

The Barton's had hoped to live on the farm until they died, but several years ago, Don said his wife started hinting that the fellow she'd married was pretty old and she didn't want to get stuck out there, so they sold the farm and moved into town. The challenges of caring for a disabled daughter and the constant struggle of farm life served to draw the couple closer. Melba Jeanne said, "Don has the most patience of anybody I've ever known." And she discovered a wonderful benefit to being a farmer's wife. "On the farm your husband is never far away. We've always done everything together."

LOVE LESSON
"When you get married, you stay married."—Don Barton

DON AND MELBA JEANNE BARTON, 2010.

Don Barton died December 6, 2013

CHAPTER 17
PIN CURLS AND ALL

MARY BRICKNER AND ROY GRAYHEK (ON LEFT),
SECOND DATE, 1946.

🎵 *If You Could See Me Now*
—TADD DAMERON & CARL SIGMAN, 1946

If Mary Bricker had let vanity rule the day, she might never have met her future husband. In 1946, Mary worked in an office at the Bremerton Shipyard and lived in a nearby dormitory for single ladies. One February evening, her friend Cora knocked on her door. Cora had a date with her boyfriend, but he didn't have a car. So, the resourceful young man found a fellow Marine, Roy Grayhek, who had one and asked him if he'd be interested in going on double date.

"I said, 'How am I going to do that? I don't know anybody,'" Roy recalled. His friend told him not to worry, assuring him that Cora would fix him up. But Cora had problems finding an available girl. She'd knocked on several doors before trying Mary's, and Mary wasn't interested either. "I'd just shampooed my hair and put it up in pin curls," Mary said. "But Cora begged me. Finally, I put on a turban and wound it over the pin curls and out we went."

ROY GRAYHEK

Roy had recently returned to Bremerton after spending three years in the South Pacific, having joined the Marines in 1940 at age 18. His reason for enlisting was simple. "I was living in Pendleton (Oregon) with no prospects of a decent job and no way to go to college." Not one to shy away from a challenge, Roy volunteered for the elite Marine Raiders in October of 1942. He served in the 4th Raider Battalion under the command of Lt. Col. James Roosevelt (President Franklin Roosevelt's oldest son) throughout the Pacific theater. The Raider battalions, organized in January 1942 and disbanded two years later, were developed as a Marine Corps special mission force.

In 1943, Roy set off for Guadalcanal aboard the USS *Polk*. From the ship, he and his fellow Marines would scramble down landing nets into waiting boats. They went from island to island throughout the Solomons, engaging the Japanese in fierce jungle combat. One particular skirmish stands out—the battle of Bairoko Harbor on the island of New Georgia, July 20, 1943. "I guess you might say we were outmanned," Roy recalled. "They started lobbing mortars at us the minute we hit the beach."

Leaning forward in his chair, he paused and frowned. "I've never talked about this before." Taking a deep breath, he continued. "I leaned my head against a tree for a moment and a bullet ricocheted off it." He rubbed his thumb down the side of his face. "A splinter hit my cheek." The next day as he sat on a tree stump, he glanced down at his feet. "I saw a bullet had torn through the sole of my boot." Roy reflected on the fate of his fellow Marines. "My machine gun squad had two killed and one badly wounded." He shook his head. "It just wasn't my time to go, that's all."

That's not to say he escaped unscathed. In addition to his shrapnel wound, months of jungle fighting resulted in a prolonged struggle with malaria and hookworm. Roy spent three months hospitalized in New Zealand before he was sent back to his ship. By the time they docked in Bremerton, Roy was ready to put the war behind him and get on with life. A blind date seemed far removed from the horror of the jungle and that suited him just fine.

The foursome went dancing. Mary said, "I thought he looked so strong and nice in his uniform."

She assumed Roy had enjoyed her company, but when he didn't call, she wondered. "I didn't call her for a few days and my buddy told me Cora said Mary were upset that I didn't call her—so I did." Turned out he just needed some prompting. Mary laughed. She already had a boyfriend and wasn't really worried, but said, "I thought maybe I didn't look so great in the turban and I wanted another chance to show him how I fixed myself up!"

Evidently, that second chance left a lasting impression because a few weeks later Roy proposed. The details, however, are vague. "I think I just said, 'Well, heck, why don't we get married?' I guess I loved her. She was beautiful!" Roy said. Then he grinned. "I'm not known for romance." Romantic or not, Mary's erstwhile beau was history, and she accepted Roy's proposal. "I just wanted to be with him," she said. On May 25, 1946, six weeks after that first date, they were married in the Naval Chapel.

When Roy was discharged in November, the couple moved to be near Roy's parents. He took a job as a lineman for Pacific Northwest Bell and stayed with the company for 40 years. In 1950 their son Stephen was born, followed by a

GRAYHEK WEDDING,
MAY 25, 1946.

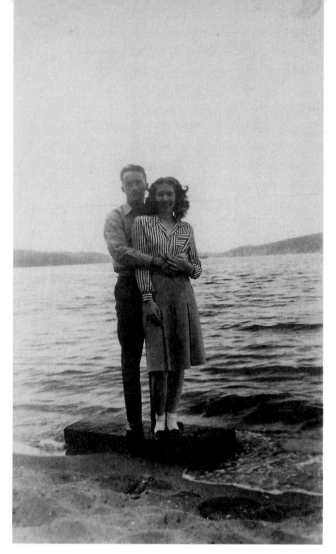

GRAYHEK HONEYMOON, JUNE 1946.

daughter, Diane, in 1951. Two years later, Roy began building a home for his family. "We lived in the basement for three years while Roy worked on the house," said Mary. "He did everything himself, except for the plumbing and brick work."

Roy shrugged. "My dad was a very good carpenter. He'd come over on the weekends and help and then lay out my work for the next week." And while Roy built the house, his family continued to grow. A son, Larry, was born in 1955, followed by another son, Paul, in 1956. Mary said, "The boys were born while we were still living in the basement—I was anxious to get out!" The house was finished in time for the arrival of Theresa in

1959, Marie in 1962 and twin girls in 1964. Sadly, one of the twins lived only eight days, but the family drew comfort from the presence of the surviving baby, Jan. The babies were the first set of twins born at Holy Family Hospital, and when Jan started school, Mary returned to the hospital—this time as a nurse's aide in the pediatrics unit.

The couple raised their bustling brood in a neighborhood filled with similar families. Neighborhood sledding parties and picnics were common, and the families often swapped babysitting duties if a couple wanted to go out. Mary sighed. "In those days you didn't fear when your kids were out of your sight."

In 1986, Roy retired from the phone company and two years later Mary retired from Holy Family. They embraced retirement with the same enthusiasm they had parenting, and embarked on a series of cross-country car trips. "She's the navigator, I'm the pilot," said Ray. But they didn't limit their travels to the U.S. They took several cruises and traveled to Germany and Japan. For Roy, the trip to Japan was a return visit. "Our outfit was the first to land in Japan and 49 years later I ended up in the same place." He shook his head. "I didn't recognize a darn thing!"

They also enjoy gardening. Roy said, "She does the flowers, I do the veggies."

His Purple Heart and three Bronze Stars are tucked away somewhere, but photos of his children and grandchildren are prominently displayed.

As they celebrate more than six decades of marriage, Mary feels like a blessed woman. "He's just a wonderful man. He knows my quirks and puts up with them." Roy added, "Yeah, but I don't talk about them!" They laughed together and reflected on the date that almost wasn't. If someone else had been willing to go—if Mary had been too vain to go out with her hair in pin curls . . . if . . .

It's something that Roy doesn't dwell on. Instead he revels in his good fortune. He said, "I was just a dumb 23-year-old—not too bright. I say the good Lord picked her out for me."

LOVE LESSON

"Be considerate and respectful of each other, but don't forget to have some joy and laugh a little."—Mary Grayhek

MARY AND ROY GRAYHEK, 2011.

Roy Grayhek died February 11, 2014

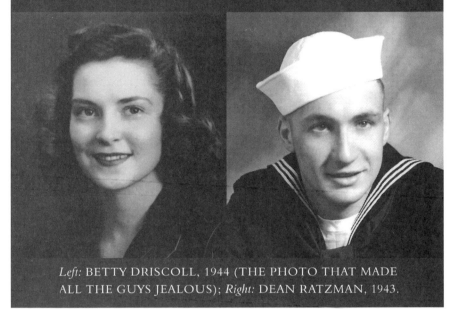

CHAPTER 18
LETTERS FROM HOME

Left: BETTY DRISCOLL, 1944 (THE PHOTO THAT MADE
ALL THE GUYS JEALOUS); *Right:* DEAN RATZMAN, 1943.

🌿 *Love Letters* — VICTOR YOUNG & EDWARD HEYMAN, 1945

A phone call from a stranger one spring evening forever changed Betty Driscoll's life. It was 1943, and the 18-year-old college freshman answered the phone. That's when a man she'd never met had the audacity to ask her for a date.

That young man was Dean Ratzman. He explained, "I was a pledge in a frat at Washington State University. We did this thing called the 'Pledge Sneak,' and a few of us rented a room in Spokane at the Davenport Hotel." Being from Tacoma, he didn't know any local girls, so before he left the campus he asked his chemistry partner for the names and phones numbers of some of her friends. Once the frat pledges arrived in Spokane, Dean began to work his way down the list. "I called Betty, and we visited. She said she wouldn't go anywhere with me alone, but she called some girlfriends and we all went to a movie."

While the date proved memorable for Betty—the movie did not. "We went to see Cat People," she said. "I was very farsighted and I'd just gotten my glasses, but I didn't put them on." Unfortunately, the only seats available were in the front row. "I sat through the whole movie with my neck back and my eyes closed," she said. Periodically, Dean whispered movie updates to her.

"I thought she was very pretty," he said. "I definitely was more interested in her than she was in me." He cleared his throat and grinned. "She told me not to get my hopes up." He also didn't have a car, which made long-distance dating difficult. Betty, a freshman at Holy Names College, was still attached to her high school sweetheart. He was away attending officer's training school, but they corresponded regularly.

In the fall of 1943, Dean enlisted in the Navy and was sent to Farragut Naval Base. He chose the Navy because his father had served in the infantry during World War I and told him, "Whatever you do, don't do that!" Betty may have discouraged him, but he didn't quite get the message. "I told her on our second date, 'I guess you know I love you.'"

She didn't take him seriously. Shaking her head, she said, "At the time I thought it was another line from a sailor!" While on a short leave, that

sailor showed up at her parent's home. The surprise visit worked out well for him. He grinned. "They invited me in for dinner!"

Soon, Dean left for California and then shipped out to the Central Pacific. Throughout his tour of duty, Betty wrote to him. She also sent a picture that Dean said made the other sailors jealous. "I hung it over my bunk and the fellas would come by and say, 'That's a beautiful girl!'" he said. "In fact, we'd compare all our girl's pictures and mine was always the prettiest." But it was her letters that kept the young man, far from home, from feeling too lonely. "Betty is a great letter writer," he said. "Her letters were a highlight for me—but I didn't know who else she was writing to." He shot her a sideways glance. "She was very patriotic."

Laughing, he recalled her frequent mention of someone named Rusty. "I thought it was her brother, but it turned out it was her dog!"

He needed that connection to home and normal life, as Dean was about to become part of the invasion of the Marianas. In particular, the island of Saipan was of great strategic importance. American forces wanted to use it as an air base to launch B-29 bombers directly at Japanese islands. After eight

Opposite page: DEAN RATZMAN (TOP ROW, 6TH FROM RIGHT), WITH HIS UNIT, 1944, SAIPAN.

DEAN RATZMAN (SHIRTLESS), 1945, SAIPAN.

weeks of brutal fighting, 60,000 Japanese ground troops and most of the carrier air power of the Japanese Imperial Navy was destroyed. Thousands of American troops perished, as well.

Dean shook his head and sighed. "The invasion of Saipan happened a little more than a week after D-Day. Thousands and thousands of people died, but there's no talk of it." He rubbed his hand across his head. "Everyone just recalls D-Day." While Dean wasn't injured during the invasion, his health still took a beating. He contracted dengue fever several times during his stint in the islands. While in Saipan he got a hernia from lifting a large battery, and following surgery, he was sent to a hospital ship, the USS *Sanctuary*. There he received some startling news—doctors aboard ship discovered Dean's heart had been damaged during his bouts with fever.

When the ship docked in Oakland, physicians at the naval hospital diagnosed the 20-year-old sailor with two leaky heart valves. "The doctors said there wasn't anything they could do," Dean recalled. "They told me I probably wouldn't live past middle age." From Oakland, he called Betty to tell her that he'd been given the option to recuperate at any military hospital. "I asked her about Farragut and she said that was a good idea." He smiled. "My heart leapt. I thought maybe I had a shot."

They quickly reconnected and their budding relationship flourished. In February 1946, Dean was discharged. Once again, he showed up at Betty's home for a family dinner—but this time, he said, "I had a ring in my pocket." He couldn't wait to pop the question and ended up proposing in the kitchen.

Betty laughed. "He's very impulsive!"

He was undeterred when Betty's aunt walked into the kitchen in the middle of his romantic speech. Dean had fallen deeply in love with Betty through her letters. "You can find so much more about someone in letters." He'd grown to love her family, too. "I was from a broken home and she had this wonderful, close-knit family." Her family liked him, but they were a bit overwhelmed by his boisterous spirit. "I'm a type-A personality and her family was all so quiet!'

Betty recalled his proposal. "He told me the doctors said he wouldn't live past 40. Then he asked me to marry him! I told him, 'You're not going to get out of it that easily!'"

Almost seven decades later, she smiled at her husband. "When you're

20, 40 seems like forever. I figured I'd get another one (husband) after that." During their engagement Dean attended classes at WSU and Betty taught at the Benewah School in rural Idaho. "I taught 31 children in eight grades," she recalled. "There was no running water. My uncle cut wood for the school and for the teacherage, which was just a tiny one-room shack."

Dean laughed. "She weighed about 98 pounds. She had 8th grade girls bigger than she was!" Betty shook her head at the memory. "I was ready to get married." Her husband nudged her shoulder. "Marrying a penniless, disabled sailor was more appealing than returning to Benewah School!"

RATZMAN WEDDING, JUNE 23, 1946.

They wed on June 23, 1946. Immediately after the wedding, they returned to Pullman because Dean had class the next day. Betty glanced at her husband. "I'm waiting for my honeymoon," she said. In 1947, their son Michael was born, and soon the family moved to Missoula, Montana where Dean graduated from law school at Montana State University. A daughter, Celia, arrived in 1949 and a second son, Steve, completed the family in 1956.

Dean took a job with Bonneville Power Administration and eventually became a supervising attorney for the U.S. Department of the Interior. That position led to an appointment as Chairman of the U.S. Department of the Interior's board of contract appeals, which necessitated a move to Virginia. "On the weekends we explored the Civil War battlefields," Dean said. "Our youngest didn't have to read about history—he experienced it."

Dean later accepted an appointment as a U.S. administrative law judge and the family moved to Sacramento. When he retired from that position in 1981, he and Betty returned to Washington. "Her family had become my family," said Dean. "Her father called me the son he never had—we were great friends and fishing partners."

While living in Virginia, Betty discovered an abiding passion for genealogy. The couple has twice traveled to England and Ireland, exploring their family history. "She's so intelligent," said Dean. "I've been amazed through the years about what she knows and what she can recall."

He may still be impulsive, but his wife said, "I've always appreciated that he lets me be me. I'm unusual—I can entertain myself quite well." Dean smiled at her. "She's not a pushover!"

As for his expected short life span, he's still going strong, though he has undergone several heart surgeries. And after 68 years marriage, Betty remains glad she answered that phone call from a stranger. She reached over and took Dean's hand. "He's a great man."

LOVE LESSON
"Everybody can have a difference of opinion—but don't stay disappointed in each other for any long period."—Dean Ratzman

---

DEAN AND BETTY RATZMAN, 2011.

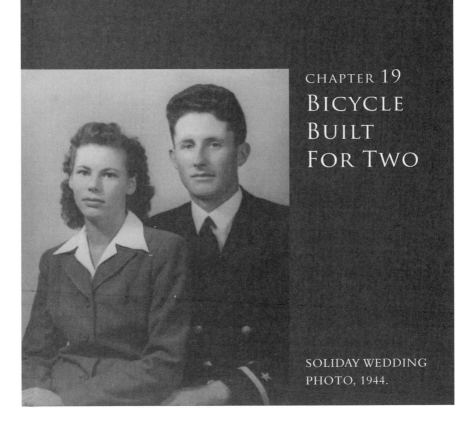

CHAPTER 19
BICYCLE
BUILT
FOR TWO

SOLIDAY WEDDING
PHOTO, 1944.

I'm Just a Lucky So-and-So
— DUKE ELLINGTON & MACK DAVID, 1945

One fellow's thirst for a beer became Chuck Soliday's lucky break. The young University of Idaho student was at a Grange dance in Moscow, Idaho, in the spring of 1941. An acquaintance had escorted a girl to the dance and didn't want to leave her alone when he snuck out to grab a beer he'd left in the car. So he introduced her to Chuck.

Chuck recently celebrated 70 years of marriage with the girl he met at that dance. "I thought, 'Boy this is it!' right away," he said, as he recalled his first sight of Harriet. "She was a good-looking girl." He didn't find the girls at college appealing. "At the University of Idaho there were four guys to every girl, and those girls were stuck up!" Glancing at Harriet, he smiled. "So, I went and got myself a high school girl!" Eighteen-year-old Harriet was friendly, sweet and a great dancer. "He got my phone number before the dance ended," she said.

Chuck, 20, didn't have a car, but that didn't hamper their dates. "He had a bicycle," said Harriet, smiling. "I'd ride on the handlebars."

SOLIDAYS CLOWNING AROUND ON THEIR HONEYMOON, FLORIDA, 1955.

They dated for more than a year before he proposed. It's not that he didn't want to pop the question sooner, but Chuck had other things on his mind. "The draft board was on my tail," he said. He really wanted to finish school, so Chuck signed up for the V-7 program offered by the Navy. "They let me finish college," he said. However, as graduation approached, he had to leave for training and wasn't able to be there to receive his diploma. Harriet gladly picked it up for him.

The Navy wouldn't allow them to marry until he finished midshipman school, in 1944. Because of the war, the Navy crammed the four-year school into four short months. "The military needed officers," he explained. When he completed his training and received his commission, he sent for Harriet, who traveled by train to Norfolk, Virginia. "I arrived at the train station. The train left. I sat there, and sat there, but he didn't come," she recalled. She shared her worries with a lady sitting next to her on the bench. When Chuck finally arrived, Harriet burst into tears and so did her new friend.

Because it was a weekend, they had difficulty getting their blood tests and obtaining a marriage license. Once they accomplished these tasks, they had to quickly find a place to marry. "We went to the YMCA and got married by a Navy chaplain," Harriet said. "We didn't have anyone to stand up with us, so the chaplain asked 'Does anyone want to witness this wedding?' and a dozen sailors eagerly volunteered."

While their wedding, on January 16, 1944, was sweet and memorable, their honeymoon was non-existent. Chuck said, "We got married on Sunday, and Monday morning I was on a troop train to Florida for heavy surf training." His bride found her own ride and rented a room in a house with

CHUCK AND HARRIET SOLIDAY ON THEIR HONEYMOON.

another officer's wife. "I was in charge of small boats and landing craft," Chuck said. "I lived in a tent out on an island, but I got to see her when I had time off." During his time off, Harriet had a chance to enjoy the sand and the surf, but mostly they just enjoyed being together.

In March he received orders to ship out overseas, and Harriet returned to Idaho to wait for his return. Chuck counts himself fortunate. "I got over there before Normandy," he said. "The Navy had planned so far ahead we had a bunch of landing craft prepared." He and his crew landed in France, practically on the Riviera. From there they traveled to Marseilles. "I was in charge of three small boats and crews."

Meanwhile, back home, Harriet waited and eagerly looked for his letters. She shook her head. After only two months with her husband, she endured a 17-month separation from him.

When Germany surrendered in 1945, Chuck finally got a 30-day leave and he and Harriet had a joyous reunion. "While I was on leave they dropped the bomb (on Hiroshima)," he said. "If it hadn't been for that I would have been on board a ship, ready to invade Japan." Instead, he was sent back to Norfolk to train other officers, and then returned to civilian life.

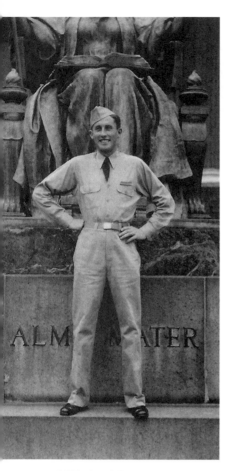

CHUCK SOLIDAY AT
COLUMBIA UNIVERSITY
FOR OTS.

Back in Moscow he enrolled in one semester of college. "Just to get my head back into architecture—it had been awhile!" In 1946 they welcomed a son. "We finally got into vet's housing," said Harriet. "It was like a whole bunch of little apartments stuck together." Chuck took a job with an architectural firm in Idaho Falls, and soon after moving, their family expanded with the birth of a daughter.

After nine years in Idaho Falls, a new job took them to Washington state where another son was born. "Every time we moved she got pregnant," Chuck said. "So when we moved to Spokane in 1955, I said, 'We'd better stop moving!'" Even with a houseful of kids, they always made time to dance—after all, dancing brought them together in the first place. "We just loved square dancing," Harriet said. "We belonged to five or six groups." She delighted in sewing her costumes with full skirts and colorful blouses.

Their talents weren't confined to do-si-do's. They also became excellent ballroom dancers and joined a couple of dance clubs. While Harriet favors the waltz, Chuck is partial to the samba. "We had a routine for that," he said, snapping his fingers and swaying to a tune he hummed.

When he retired in 1988, the couple enjoyed traveling both at home and abroad. They visited Sweden twice, and on one memorable trip they visited seven countries by bus. Regular bridge games kept them mentally sharp, and Chuck golfed into his 80's. Their family now includes seven grandchildren and six great grandchildren. "It's a happy bunch," said Chuck.

They attribute the longevity of their marriage to working well together. "It's quite a thing to stay married this long," said Chuck. "I'm proud of that." They share the household chores. "He vacuums and makes the bed," said

Harriet. "And he drives me to my hair appointment every week."

She reached out and took her husband's hand. "We get along good," she said. "And I get a goodnight kiss every night."

LOVE LESSON

"We help each other a lot. Working together makes life easier."—Harriet Soliday

---

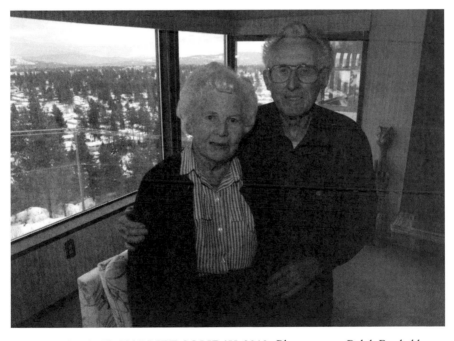

CHUCK AND HARRIET SOLIDAY, 2010. *Photo courtesy Ralph Bartholdt*

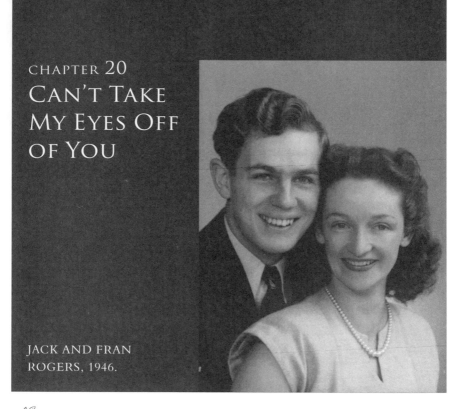

CHAPTER 20

CAN'T TAKE MY EYES OFF OF YOU

JACK AND FRAN
ROGERS, 1946.

🌿 *A Lovely Way to Spend an Evening*
—JIMMY MCHUGH & HAROLD ADAMSON, 1943

When Jack Rogers walked into a friend's home, she was the first thing he saw. She wore a blue dress with big spools of thread printed on the fabric and she sat on the floor next to the fireplace. He couldn't take his eyes off of her. Fran Rogers also remembers her first sight of Jack. "He was beautiful," she said with a sigh. "He had a golden tan from the South Pacific and his hair was bleached almost white from the sun."

More than six decades after that first glimpse of each other, the couple still smiles at the memory. They went to the local skating rink that night. Fran had been trying to learn, but Jack's skating skills were polished. "He was a beautiful skater," she recalled. "And I was not. I was still hanging on to the walls." Yet Jack didn't want to skate with anyone else. "I just skated backwards, if I recall," he said.

A month later he proposed and two months later, they married. "It was a long engagement of three months," said Jack, grinning. "I was convinced from the first day that she had it all. She just fit what I was looking for." Fran believes that Jack, like many soldiers returning from World War II, felt like he'd already lost three years of his life and didn't want to lose any more time.

In 1943, at age 19, Jack had enlisted in the Army. "Most of the kids I went to school with at Roosevelt High, in Seattle, enlisted." He found it difficult to believe we were at war against Japan. "I grew up with a bunch of Japanese kids," he said, shaking his head. Jack even traveled to California to see a buddy from his high school tumbling team, only to find his friend and his family had been placed in an internment camp. Later that buddy worked as an interpreter for the Army.

Jack was assigned to the amphibious engineers unit and spent three years on active duty, most of it spent in the Philippines and as part of the occupational forces in Japan. "Our whole company was made up of kids—kids dressed up as soldiers," he said. "At 19, I was in charge of 55 men." He shrugged. "You grew into the job." His outfit was the first one back into Manila, Philippines, after Gen. Douglas MacArthur's famous landing. They were torpedoed by subs and shot at by kamikazes, but Jack was able to find some humor in the midst of the horror.

One day in particular stands out. "We'd traveled all day down the Cagayan River to meet up with an anti-tank crew," Jack recalled. Night fell and they couldn't see a thing, so they made the decision to drop anchor and wait it out.

"Japs were on both sides of the river. We waited all night for a hand grenade to be tossed. The next morning we resumed our journey and found our destination was just around the bend, less than 100 yards away!"

JACK ROGERS, HOME ON LEAVE, 1943.

JACK ROGERS, NEW GUINEA, 1943.

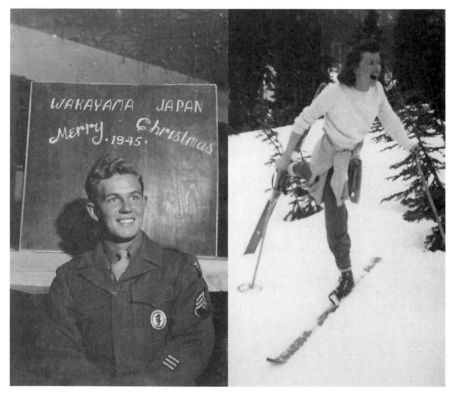

JACK ROGERS,
CHRISTMAS 1945.

FRAN, ENGAGEMENT DAY
AT STEVENS PASS, 1946.

Then one night in 1945 an officer came up to Jack and said, "They just announced that the war is over—but hold your positions because the Japanese aren't convinced." The rumor spread and the troops grew excited. The following morning the same officer returned. "False alarm!" he said.

But for every humorous story there are memories of being scared, alone, and far from home—memories of hundreds of bodies left on streets and beaches by the retreating Japanese forces. Jack grimaced. "It was pretty rough. In some cases we had to push the bodies aside with bulldozers." That's why he didn't waste any time when he met Fran. "He just wanted a family because he'd never really had one," said Fran. Jack nodded. "I lived in a boarding house 'til I was eight. I'd never seen my father."

One February day, Jack and Fran set off with two other couples for a day of skiing at Steven's Pass. "Six of us traveled in a tiny coupe," Fran said. "In fact, I was sitting on Jack's lap when he whispered in my ear, 'I really think we ought to get married, don't you?'"

So, on April 26, 1946, they married in the house where they met. Jack found work as a carpenter and soon they found some property. "I built a tiny little house with second hand materials," he said. On December 26 they welcomed their first child. "He was a preemie and weighed less than five pounds," Fran recalled. "When we brought him home the neighbor lady looked at him and said, 'Boy, you'll never raise that one.'"

She was wrong, and in 1949 a second son joined their family. They struggled financially. Jack said he took every job he could find, often working two or three jobs at a time. A trip to California to visit an old friend proved providential. The friend was a commercial artist and Jack said, "That's what I want to do." Jack had always been artistic. When he was nine he sold his first piece, a drawing of an alligator swallowing a donkey, for $5. While working and raising a family, he attended the Carnegie Institute in Seattle and got hired by a large company before he'd even graduated. Eventually, a local advertising company recruited him to Spokane. Jack agreed to come for a year, and has been here ever since. It was a move his wife has never been happy about. "I love Seattle and LA," she said. "There's so much more to see."

Jack cleared his throat and grinned. "She was very cordial about the whole thing."

The birth of a daughter in 1953 made life even busier for Fran, and Jack expanded his horizons as well. In 1963 he was asked to help start the art department at Spokane Falls Community College, where he ended up teaching for 26 years.

Fran went to work for JC Penny when their youngest started school, and was named a department manager at a time when few women achieved that position. But their lives took an unexpected turn when, at age 46, Fran found out she was expecting another child. Their daughter was 17, and their sons grown and gone. The news came as quite a shock and the doctors were concerned. "They thought something was wrong with the baby," Fran said quietly. "There was no movement."

So she did the only thing she could think of—she prayed. "I asked God, 'If this baby is alive, would you please save it?'" Her eyes filled with tears at the memory. "And the baby kicked me." She gave birth to a healthy daughter on March 3, 1970. "Our lives started over again," she with an eloquent shrug. Not only did they raise their surprise baby, but they also raised their granddaughter, Jennifer, from the time she was three.

"We've had 58 years of nonstop parenting," Fran said. Yet the couple recently completed Bloomsday, an annual 12 kilometer timed road race. Jack has never missed a race and this year Fran wanted to walk it with him, even though she'd recently had knee replacement surgery. It was harder than she'd anticipated, but Jack held her hand the entire way. "The last two miles, I leaned on him," she admitted. But she wouldn't quit. "I have to finish everything I start," she said.

The best marital advice they offer is to stay busy and take care of your health. The active couple has backpacked, skied and worked out together for most of their married life. Though they've had differences, divorce was never an option. "We never had enough money to get a divorce," said Fran with a twinkle in her eye. "And nobody wanted to get stuck with the kids!"

She threw back her head and laughed. Across the table Jack smiled and watched. He still can't take his eyes off her.

LOVE LESSON
"Never retire!"—Jack Rogers, 90
"Stay healthy! We work out three to four times a week."—Fran Rogers, 91

JACK AND FRAN ROGERS, 2011. *Photo courtesy Ralph Bartholdt*

CHAPTER 21

HAPPY
TRAILS

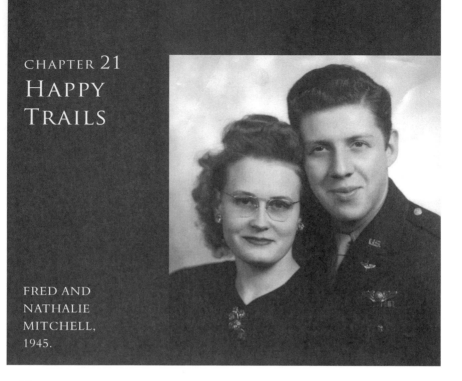

FRED AND
NATHALIE
MITCHELL,
1945.

Trav'lin' Light
— TRUMMY YOUNG, JIMMY MUNDAY & JOHNNY MERCER, 1942

I f Fred Mitchell hadn't been at the Greyhound bus station in Sioux Falls, South Dakota in the summer of 1944, he might never have met the love of his life. A beautiful girl, wearing a saucy white hat, had just stepped off the bus and looked around for her boyfriend who was supposed to meet her. "A whole bunch of soldiers were waiting around to see who got off the bus," Nathalie Mitchell recalled.

"And I was one of them," said Fred.

Nathalie's boyfriend, however, was not.

Fred struck up a conversation with her and kept her company while she waited. "She was a good looking gal," he said. When her boyfriend didn't show, he offered to call a cab and see her home. She accepted and before she got out of the taxi, he had her phone number. "It must have been that cute little white hat," she mused. Whatever the reason, Fred wasted no time in giving her a call and inviting her to dinner and a movie. She agreed to the date and never looked back. "So much for that boyfriend," Fred said, chuckling.

Fred was anxious to move on with his life. He'd recently returned to the States after serving with the 452nd Air Bomb Group stationed in England. He'd been attending Purdue University, in 1943, when the Army Air Force called his name. "I'd never even been up in a plane—I'd never flown," he said. So, he thought it best to apply for navigation training.

He flew 30 missions between January and April of 1945, mostly over Germany. "We got shot up all the time," he said, shaking his head. During one memorable incident, while seated in his spot in the nose of the B-17, a big piece of shrapnel struck the plane. "It hit the Plexiglass and shattered it. I thought it was snowing!" After Germany surrendered, Fred and his crew had a new mission picking up POW's in Czechoslovakia and flying them home. "They were mainly French," he recalled. "And when we flew past the Eiffel Tower, boy did they get excited!"

He hadn't yet decided his future career plans when he met Nathalie at the bus station, but he knew immediately that whatever his future held, he wanted her by his side. "We probably dated a whole month before I asked her to marry me," he said. "And once she agreed, I decided to stay in the service." He applied for pilot training and was sent to Walla Walla, Washington. Nathalie soon followed him, and on November 30, 1945 they married in a local pastor's home.

They didn't stay in Washington long. By October of 1946, Fred and his bride were in San Angelo, Texas, where he attended flight school. While there, they welcomed the birth of David, the first of three sons. From Texas they went to Louisiana so Fred could complete his advanced training in B-25's. The frequent moves suited Nathalie perfectly. She's always enjoyed being on the go. "When I was a baby my mother would take me out in the buggy every afternoon,"

FRED MITCHELL, GUNNERY SCHOOL, FLORIDA, 1944.

FRED MITCHELL TOOK THIS PICTURE OF A B-17
DROPPING ITS PAYLOAD OVER GERMANY, 1945.

FRED MITCHELL, HOME
ON LEAVE AFTER
NAVIGATION SCHOOL.

she said, laughing. "I loved it and wanted
to go right back out! I still love travel."
Housing was in short supply, and Fred's
solution proved fitting. He said, "I picked
up a Liberty Travel Trailer, so we'd have
a place to live."

In 1949, Fred completed weather
forecasting school and soon received orders to move his family to the Philippines, and once again Nathalie proved to
be an intrepid traveler. She and their two
sons boarded the last boat going to the
Philippines prior to the onset of the Korean War. "We went through a typhoon,"
she said. "But I never got seasick."

Their third son arrived while they
were stationed in the Philippines. The
Mitchells moved 15 times during Fred's
21-year military career, but despite all
those transfers they were rarely sepa-

rated. "I think the longest we spent apart was probably three months," Nathalie said.

After retiring from the Air Force as a major, Fred attended Great Falls College in Montana and earned a degree in education. In 1964 he launched his next career, teaching middle school and high school math in North Idaho. Nathalie said, "We found a beautiful house. It was run down but nothing we couldn't fix up." At last the Mitchells were able to put down roots, and for 21 years Fred taught a variety of math classes before retiring in 1985.

Fred's definition of retirement might be different than some—for the past 23 years he's volunteered with the AARP as a tax preparer. "I helped prepare 106 income tax returns this year," he said. Every January, he's required to take an extensive course and pass a grueling test in order to keep current with tax changes. In 2010, the couple received a Community Service award from the AARP's Retired Educators Association. A letter from the organization said, "Your efforts have enriched the lives of friends and neighbors and made your community a better place in which to live." The couple is also active in their church. Fred plays the keyboard and Nathalie makes baptismal banners. "Church has always been part of the fabric of our family," she said.

And they are still on the go. Every other summer they take a long road trip. "No planning, we just go," said Fred. "We love seeing new places." Age has caused them to modify their travel style a bit, by taking turns driving and making lots of stops along the way. In addition, they both exercise every day. Nathalie said, "That's what keeps us going!"

When asked what keeps a marriage going, they looked at each other and smiled. "He gives me what I want and lets me go where I want," Nathalie said. Fred added, "And of course, I don't argue!" He grinned and continued, "She's a good cook and took great care of the kids."

Nathalie cleared her throat. "And what about you?"

He grinned. "And me, too!" His wife reached across the table and gently patted his hand. Whirlwind courtship aside, she's happy she accepted his offer of marriage. "I thought it was a good deal."

And it has been. If she ever finds that long-ago boyfriend who missed her bus, she'd thank him. Because of his mistake, Fred and Nathalie Mitchell have enjoyed 69 years of happy trails.

LOVE LESSON
"I get the last word and that's that!"—Nathalie Mitchell

FRED AND NATHALIE MITCHELL, 2010. *Photo courtesy Ralph Bartholdt*

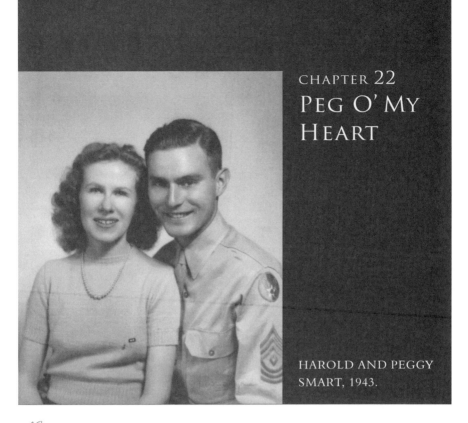

HAROLD AND PEGGY
SMART, 1943.

I Don't Want to Set the World On Fire — EDDIE SEILER,
SOL MARCUS, BENNIE BENJAMIN & EDDIE DURHAM, 1941

Peggy and Harold Smart celebrate two anniversaries—the day they married and the Fourth of July. They met in high school, and though Harold was an older man, he thought he'd have a chance with the beautiful Peggy. "I am 39 days her senior," he confided. On July 4, 1939, he seized the opportunity to be with her. They went on a double date to an open-air tea garden followed by fireworks at Natatorium Park in Spokane, Washington.

"After that," Harold said, "she didn't go out with another guy and I didn't go out with another girl." Natatorium Park also featured prominently in one of their most memorable dates. "The Nat" began as a trolley park— a destination at the end of the trolley line to give passengers a reason to keep riding. In addition to amusement park rides, a zoo, and the state's first heated swimming pool, the park had a first-class dance pavilion which attracted bands and performers from across the nation.

One night Harold took Peggy to The Nat to hear Kay Kyser and his band. "He liked to dance more than I did," Peggy said. "He grew up in the country and went to Grange dances every Saturday." That evening their date took an unexpected twist. "We were dancing and all of a sudden there was a huge 'BAM!'" Harold recalled. A portion of the dance floor collapsed. "We rode it down," he said, chuckling. "The floor sloped down to the sunken part. One of the supports had given way." That didn't deter their date. After someone came and checked out the damage, they were given the go-ahead to resume dancing—they just skirted the sunken area.

Though they enjoyed spending time together, unfortunately, their courtship faced a transportation issue: Harold didn't own a car. He quickly grew tired of borrowing one so he could take his girl out. "I had to get one. I was desperate!" he said. "I bought a 1933 Chevy."

After graduation, they both continued their education, she at secretarial school, he at a local business university. Harold said, "There wasn't any thought of marriage. Neither of us could afford to pay the light bill." And soon, war interrupted all talk of future plans. "In August 1942, I got called up by the Army."

HAROLD SMART, 1943.

He and Peggy fell quiet as they recalled the day the draft notice came. They gazed out of their window at the rolling Palouse hills of Pullman, Washington. Peggy sighed. "It wasn't a surprise. We knew it was coming." Harold left for Ft. Douglas, Utah, but when his superiors learned he could type, his time in basic training was cut short. He mused, "Isn't it something, how one little thing can change your whole life?"

In fact, Harold believes his typing skills may have saved his life—it certainly kept him off the front lines. Being handy at the typewriter also moved him quickly up the ranks, making first sergeant within six months. "My pay went from $50 a month to $138!" With his newfound wealth he purchased an engagement ring for Peggy and sent it to her in the mail. Neither could recall a formal proposal. "It was just assumed we'd marry," said Harold.

Peggy laughed. "Apparently, I agreed."

Glancing at Harold, she continued. "We didn't even consider a big wedding." She joined her groom in South Carolina, and on March 14, 1943, they were married by the chaplain in an Army chapel. "I had a man bridesmaid," she said. "There were no women there." Their honeymoon was spent moving from base to base. "We had the best honeymoon anybody ever had," said Peggy. For her, just being with Harold was better than any exotic trip.

When he was transferred to Florida, Peggy rode the troop train with a few other wives. Though their husbands were in a different compartment, Harold managed to find his bride and even brought her lunch. "He gave me a bologna sandwich and some fruit cocktail," she recalled. They enjoyed six months of togetherness before word came that Harold would be sent overseas. "I closed up the little apartment we had in Florida and got a train ticket back home," she said. "We said goodbye not knowing when or if we'd see each other again."

Harold counted off the bodies of water he eventually crossed. "The Atlantic, the Mediterranean, the Suez Canal, the Red Sea, the Indian Ocean and the Pacific." And he wasn't even a sailor!

Three long years would pass without sight of his wife or his country. After a stop in North Africa, Harold and the 1575th Ordnance Supply and Maintenance Company arrived in Bombay, India, on February 1, 1944—his 23rd birthday. Letters written daily flew back and forth between him and his bride. "I looked forward to those letters," he said.

PEGGY SMART, 1944.

Peggy glanced at him and softly asked, "What else did he have?"

But those letters are now long gone. "We didn't save any of them—those were private," Peggy explained. Harold kept a picture of her in his sleeping quarters in India, and later, when the war was over, he introduced his bunkmate to Peggy. Harold laughed at the memory. "He said, 'I *know* Peggy! I said good morning to her every day!'" When she got word he was finally coming home, she said, "I bought some steaks and took a train to Seattle." But Harold ended up in San Pedro. "I was so disappointed." Back home she went, until she was finally notified he'd be arriving in Seattle. They were eventually reunited in February 1946. She wasn't crazy about the hotel room she'd found for them, but Harold didn't mind it a bit. After years of barracks life he said, "I thought it seemed grand."

Unlike many returning soldiers, Harold had no problem finding a job—thanks to his wife. At the time, Peggy was working for the Washington Surveying & Rating Bureau, where she regaled her bosses and contacts with tales of her wonderful husband. "The guys looked forward to her updates," Harold said. "They asked, 'You don't suppose Harold would be interested in a job here?'" Indeed he was, and arrived for an interview in his uniform. "That's all the clothes he had!" Peggy said. He was hired on the spot.

They welcomed daughter Judy in 1949, and another daughter, Janet, completed their family in 1952. Harold enjoyed a long career in the insurance industry. "His parents brought him up the way my parents brought me up. You worked hard—did what you could, and didn't worry that you weren't setting the world on fire," Peggy said. "I was married to a traveling man right from the start. My dad traveled a lot, so I was used to it."

In spite of his time on the road, they maintained an active social life—or tried to. "The worst part of his traveling is we were trying to learn bridge," she said. They had a bridge party every Friday—the day Harold would finally return home from his week on the road. They had a scant few hours to change and head out. Peggy said, "We never did learn bridge."

After 20 years as a partner in the Downen Insurance Agency, where Peggy also worked, Harold retired in 1986. "Well, theoretically, I retired," he said. "I just went to board meetings," He chuckled. "They pretend I'm important."

With age, their roles have changed a bit. Peggy's health has declined, so Harold is trying to learn his way around the kitchen. "He keeps things going," she said. They still enjoy celebrating the anniversary of their first date every July 4th.

And more than seven decades later, Harold still can't believe his luck. He pointed to the picture he'd kept beside his bunk during the war. "I look at her and think, boy, how did I ever get a girl like that?"

LOVE LESSON

"You have to have a lot of love and appreciation for each other."—Harold Smart

---

HAROLD AND PEGGY SMART, 2011.

Peggy died September 5, 2013

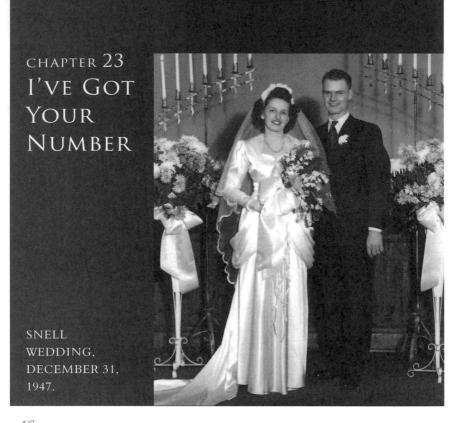

🌿 *Blue Eyes Crying in the Rain* — FRED ROSE, 1945

Bob Snell knows how to seize a moment. In December 1946, he and a friend attended a dance at the Half Moon Grange, where he spotted Demaris (Dee) Brooks. "She was with another guy," recalled Bob. But when her date left to use the restroom, Bob took advantage of his absence.

"He asked me to dance," Dee said, laughing. "I liked the other fellow, but I liked Bob better. He had big blue eyes and he was so tall and handsome." By the time her date returned to claim her, Bob had secured Dee's phone number. Or so he thought. Weeks passed and Dee wondered why her blue-eyed dance partner didn't call, but it turned out she'd given him her address and not her phone number. Undeterred, he spent hours going through the phone book, trying to match her address with a phone number. "I finally found it," he said.

His persistence had been honed during his time in the service. After graduating from high school in 1942, Bob received a draft notice. "I wanted

to join the Navy, but I flunked the color blind test, so I joined the Army."
After completing basic training, he decided to become a paratrooper. Bob
said, "My biggest motivation was greed—they doubled my salary from $50
to $100!"

He quickly found out how he'd be earning that pay. The young soldier
had never even been on an airplane, and six decades later, he shook his head
as he recalled, "On my first plane ride, they made me jump out!" With four
weeks of Jump School under his belt, Bob and his unit traveled to North
Africa. "I was there for awhile—we were kind of lost, I guess," he said,
chuckling. From there they were sent to Italy where Bob received a lasting

wartime souvenir during the Battle of
Anzio. While under heavy fire, he took
cover at the corner of a house. As he
fired his rifle, an enemy bullet penetrated
his right arm, shattering both the bones.
The date? February 16, 1944—exactly
one year since he'd been inducted.

"I guess I was lucky. I got it there,"
he said pointing to his arm, "Instead of
here," he said, and thumped his chest.
Medics set his arm in a field hospital and
Bob was sent stateside to recuperate.
His paratroop adventure was over. After
seven months and several surgeries, he
finally returned home. Due to nerve and
muscle damage, he still can't completely
unclench his right hand.

BOB SNELL (RIGHT) AND
HIS BROTHER, JOHN.

But those scars didn't stop him from
dancing with Dee. Or from asking her
out once he finally tracked down her
phone number. Their first date proved
unexpectedly memorable. "We went out to dinner," Bob said. "I ordered
fish and got a fish bone caught in my throat and started choking."

Did his date rush to his rescue? Did she call for help?

No.

Dee said, "I started laughing and I couldn't stop!" Her less than empathetic reaction didn't keep Bob from asking for a second date, and a third.

Like many post-war couples, their courtship was hampered by trans-portation issues. "I was slow on dates because I didn't have a car," he said. "I got tired of taking the bus to her house, so I finally bought a used Dodge." That car came in handy. Three months after their first date, Bob proposed to Dee as they sat in her driveway in the Dodge. "I wondered if it was a little soon," Dee said. "But I said yes, right away—I didn't want to lose him." The fact that her parents approved of him gave her added confidence.

The couple married on December 31, 1947, and rented a house for $78 a month. For many years Bob worked for Remington Rand as a typewriter repairman, and later spent 26 years working for an office equipment com-pany. In 1948 Dee gave birth to their first child, a son they named Steve. The family grew with the addition of two daughters, one in 1949 and another in 1954. And in 1964, when Steve was a senior in high school, a third daughter made a surprise appearance.

Like many parents, the Snells time with their kids at home flew by in a whirl of sporting events and school activities. An accomplished seamstress, Dee was awarded a certificate of recognition for sewing countless tiny gar-ments and donating them to a local hospital for families whose babies had been stillborn.

When Bob retired and the kids had flown the nest, the couple enjoyed traveling. Sadly, their son Steve battled melanoma and passed away at 35, but they took comfort in their growing brood of grandchildren. "Steve's son is the spitting image of his dad," Dee said.

Several years ago, grandson Jeff accompanied Bob on a trip to Italy. They revisited many of the places he'd been during the war, and Bob returned with a certificate of honor from the citizens of Anzio, which read, "The City of Anzio honors those who fought so valiantly, without fearing for their own lives on the beachhead during the battle of Anzio. Lest we forget."

"We found a few buildings that were there when I was and we went to the National Cemetery," said Bob. "I brought home a jar of sand from the beachhead." In July 2010, Bob traveled to Washington D.C. to see the World War II Memorial courtesy of the Honor Flight program. Like so many vet-erans, Bob found the flight and the memorial incredibly moving.

The Snells admit their marital seas haven't always offered smooth sail-ing. "We've had a lot of disagreements," Bob said.

Dee agreed. "We've always said what was on our minds." But her husband quickly pointed out, "We don't hold anything back. We don't have any secrets." And he's delighted that the moment he seized more than six decades ago has resulted in a lifetime love affair. When asked which years have been their happiest, Bob puzzled over the question. Finally, he looked at Dee and said, "They've all been happy."

She smiled back at him. "He's very understanding, loving and sweet. He's always been that way. I don't know what I'd do without him. Placing her timeworn hand atop his crippled fingers, she said, "We've had a wonderful life."

LOVE LESSON
"The key to our happy relationship is pretty simple—
we listen to each other."—Bob Snell

BOB AND DEE SNELL, 2010.

Dee Snell died July 6, 2012

CHAPTER 24

THE SHORT DRIVE HOME

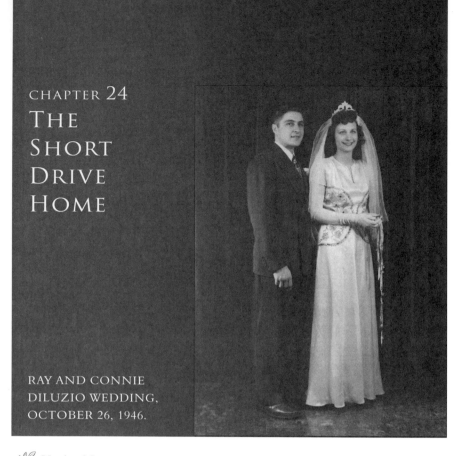

RAY AND CONNIE
DILUZIO WEDDING,
OCTOBER 26, 1946.

🍃 *You're Nearer* — RICHARD RODGERS & LORENZ HART, 1940

In 1943, Constance (Connie) Disotell saw a handsome young sailor with a shock of wavy black hair slide into a booth at the ice cream parlor where her mother worked. Though they'd never been introduced, she knew exactly who he was. Her friend had shown Connie a picture of her handsome new beau, and there Ray Diluzio sat, having ice cream with a buddy.

"I walked up to the booth and said, 'I know you!'" Connie recalled. "I was being a smart aleck. He looked up and said, 'Well, I sure don't know you!'" Yet Ray decided then and there that he definitely wanted to get to know the saucy 15-year-old beauty. When her mother closed the ice cream shop, they found Ray waiting at the curb in his dad's Model A Ford. "Would you like a ride home?" he asked.

Connie thought to herself, *Heck it's only three blocks!* But she told him, "Well, my Mom's with me . . ." To which Ray replied, "That's okay." He drove them both three blocks home, and when her mom went inside, Connie and Ray sat in the car and talked for a few minutes. "When do I get to see you again?" he asked. So she gave him her phone number.

Time was of the essence. Ray had joined the Navy in 1942, at 17, and was home on a brief leave. "I had to convince my mother to sign for me," he said. "I didn't want to get drafted and end up in the infantry." He and Connie enjoyed just few dates, but the time they spent together was enough to leave a lasting impression on both of them. And Connie's friend who carried Ray's picture? "She didn't talk much to me after that," Connie said. When it was time for Ray to return to his ship, he extracted a promise from his girl. "Please, don't date anyone else," he asked. And though she was still in high school, she agreed. It was an easy promise to keep. "I was in love with him."

RAY DILUZIO, 1943.

Ray spent 19 months in the Mediterranean and the Pacific serving aboard both the USS *Hollis* and the USS *Dixie*. "We were under a lot of fire, but we never got a direct hit," he recalled. "In the Mediterranean we got credit for sinking a submarine." The storms they endured at sea were as dangerous as enemy fire. Connie mentioned, "He saw a couple guys get washed overboard. They couldn't go back to get them." Her husband shook his head and winced at the memory.

Though his letters home were heavily censored, he found a clever way to let his parents know where he was. His parents were born in Italy, so he wrote to his mom, "Things haven't changed much since you were a kid here." Amazingly, that made it past the censors, but some correspondence came back to haunt him

RAY ABOARD
THE USS *DIXIE*.

after he and Connie married. "He'd met a couple girls back East, before I met him," Connie explained. The girls worked for Nabisco.

"They sent me all kinds of cookies and stuff," said Ray. "Boy! I looked forward to those." That was all well and good, but after they were married Ray's mother showed Connie a picture of the two girls sitting in a convertible. Clearing her throat, Connie said, "After she'd showed me that picture a couple times, I took care of it. I put it in a real safe place. So safe it disappeared." But that incident was still several years away. Connie routinely road her bicycle to his parent's house while he was overseas; she found that spending time with them eased her worries about Ray's safety. She knew, better than most, the dangers he faced. Connie's oldest brother was killed in battle during the final days of World War II.

RAY DILUZIO (RIGHT)
IN SICILY, 1944.

In between assignments, Ray had a brief leave in San Diego. "His mom and his younger brother were going to see him and he asked me to come with them," Connie said. Her dad bought her a train ticket and off she went. Seizing the opportunity, Ray proposed during her visit. Though she was in love with him, his offer of marriage came as quite a surprise to the high school junior. Connie said, "It was a shock. I wasn't thinking about getting married! I said, 'Well, let me think it over.'"

She didn't think long. The next day she told him, "Alright, fine. I will!" But when Ray pressed her to marry him before he shipped out, she said no. "I wanted to finish high school—that was uppermost." So, Ray departed for China aboard the USS *Dixie* and Connie returned to her home and her education.

In December 1945, Ray sent word that he'd soon be docking for good in Bremerton, WA. Connie was thrilled and immediately wrote a letter to his commanding officer, requesting permission for Ray to get leave to take her to her senior prom. Permission was granted. Ray and the Navy parted ways in May 1946, and on October 26, the couple wed at St. Patrick's Catholic Church. "I didn't have any money to buy a wedding dress," Connie said. "So I wore a formal with cap sleeves, and wore long white gloves because you didn't go to church with bare arms."

They lived with Ray's sister and brother-in-law for the first year of their marriage. Daughter Carol arrived September 20, 1947, and the small family set up house in an apartment in an old Army barracks. Ray worked briefly for Great Northern Railroad like his father before him, but when his dad offered to give him a corner lot on Market Street, Ray decided to start a small fruit stand. However, he didn't stop there—he soon expanded the produce stand into a grocery store complete with living quarters behind it. While he labored over the construction, he worked additional jobs to support his family, and Connie ran the store. "He built it himself," she said.

"No." Ray gently corrected her. "We did it together."

Their family grew with the birth of Ray Jr., who arrived on his dad's birthday, September 17, 1950. "It was a lot of hard work, raising two kids in the grocery store," said Connie. "I got tired. I said, 'I'm leaving this place—you'd better sell it or something.'" So after six years they leased the store to someone else, and Ray worked in food sales for a variety of companies including Kraft Foods and Golden Grain. Their family was complete with the birth of Brad in 1958.

When Ray retired at 51, he kept his connection to the food business, but in a much more hands-on way. He tended his raised bed vegetable gardens with exquisite care. Known as the "Garlic King," he grew garlic that was brought directly from Italy by his father. The original seeds were sewn into his father's coat when he arrived in the U.S., and now Ray's children grow and harvest garlic from those original seeds

In fact, the garden is one of their secrets to a happy marriage. "Sometimes, I stick myself in the kitchen and he goes out in the garden," Connie said.

She looked across the kitchen table at the fellow she first spotted at another table so many years ago. "We were young and dumb," she said. "But you learn as you go."

Ray has no complaints. He grinned and said, "I have a wonderful wife."

LOVE LESSON

"We never fight over money. We've never drawn a dime from unemployment and never bounced a check."—Ray Diluzio

RAY AND CONNIE DILUZIO, 2012.

Ray Diluzio died January 11, 2013

CHAPTER 25
THE PREACHER'S BOY AND
THE FARMER'S DAUGHTER

CLYDE AND MARY JANE, 1939.

Fools Rush in (Where Angels Fear to Tread)
— JOHNNY MERCER & RUBE BLOOM, 1940

In May 1940, Gary Cooper, Ginger Rogers and Mickey Rooney graced the covers of movie magazines; Winston Churchill became Prime Minister of Great Britain and in a tiny town in Montana, Clyde and Mary Jane Walden got married. Seven decades later, they're still smiling.

The couple met while attending high school in Montour, Idaho. "It was a very small school," said Mary Jane. "There were only eight in my graduating class." The close knit group put on a lot of plays during the year, and Clyde and Mary Jane got to know each other during the hours spent rehearsing and performing.

Clyde's father, a minister, had come to build a church in a neighboring town. Mary Jane's father, a farmer, didn't consider the ministry a "real job." As Clyde recalled, "Her dad said, 'Don't go out with that guy, 'cause he's a preacher's son.'" But the preacher's boy had already figured out how to win

WALDEN WEDDING
PHOTO, MAY 24, 1940.

the approval of the industrious farmer. "I hired on to help him work during the harvest," Clyde said. "When he saw how hard I worked, he never said another word."

When Clyde's family moved to Montana, the couple kept in touch through letters. Mary Jane said, "No phone calls—the party line invaded our privacy!" As Clyde prepared for high school graduation, his sister, Ruth, drove to Montour and picked up Mary Jane so she could attend the ceremony. "Two days after his graduation he asked me to marry him," said Mary Jane.

The next day, under an arch of wildflowers she and Ruth had gathered, Clyde and Mary Jane were married in his parents' living room. The quick wedding made sense to the couple. "We'd gone together for over two years," said Mary Jane, plus she didn't have a way to get back to Idaho. And the morning of the wedding, Clyde made sure their plans were approved by her father—he sent him a telegram requesting permission to marry. Her father telegraphed this reply: "Yes. Letter following. Love and good luck." He'd already told his daughter, "If you marry, you marry for life. You don't leave Clyde."

Their honeymoon consisted of a day-long hike in the nearby Mission Mountains—with Clyde's parents. Mary Jane said, "It was a beautiful day, but oh the ticks we brought back!"

Clyde worked six days a week at a hardware store, earning $45 a month for his labor. "It was hard," he admitted. "No money in those days." Mary Jane agreed. "We saved up all week to buy hamburger. It cost .25 for three pounds." In 1941, they welcomed their first daughter, Barbara. Mary Jane loved being a mother. "Oh, it was so fun!" she said.

Tired of the low wages at the hardware store, Clyde went to work as a fireman for Northern Pacific Railroad. He spent hours each day shoveling coal to keep the engine going, but the pay made the hard work worth it. "We were in hog heaven," he said. "It was a wonderful time. We lived it up because we hadn't had anything in so long." Often, he'd return late at night. They had no car so he'd walk from the depot to their home. "Some nights, he fell asleep on his feet and stumbled off the side of the road." Mary Jane said.

With World War II raging, Clyde tried to enlist in the military, but many railroad employees were considered essential civilian workers. "They told me they'd call me when they wanted me," he said, and shrugged.

Another daughter joined the family in 1944 and when she was 11 months old, Uncle Sam finally called. At 24, Clyde left his wife and daughters and traveled to Texas for training. Mary Jane said, "They recognized leadership quality in him and sent him to OTS (Officer Training School)."

The separation proved difficult for both of them. Missing her husband, Mary Jane and her oldest daughter traveled three days by train to Texas, leaving the baby home with family. "Clyde was on base and they wouldn't let him off, but he slipped out to meet me at the hotel. He was only there long enough to say hello, before he had to get back to base," she said. The planned short visit stretched into an entire summer. "Clyde really wanted me to stay." A local radio station was giving air time to military wives, so she went to the station and asked for a place to stay where she could be near her husband. A woman called with an offer of a room for Mary Jane and her three-year-old daughter.

In September they returned home and Clyde traveled to his next posting. He found military life rewarding. "I enjoyed training the troops very much," he said. However, during his service he witnessed a lot of racial tension—especially in Alabama and Georgia. "It was really hard on

CLYDE WALDEN, TEXAS, 1945.

me," the Northwest native admitted. Mary Jane nodded, "It was a different world down there." Though he planned to continue his service, thirty days before he and his men were to be sent overseas, the war ended and instead of going overseas, he returned to Montana.

Like his father, Clyde decided to enter the ministry and even attended the same Bible College. After ordination, the family moved to Hungry Horse, Montana, to start a church. "It was just a wilderness," Clyde recalled.

He built a little cabin for his family and later built a church on a hilltop. At his next church there was no parsonage, so the family lived in the church basement until Clyde built them a home.

For more than 20 years he pastored churches throughout the state. In 1953, a third daughter, Bonnie, completed the family. Mary Jane admitted, "There were times it was difficult raising three preacher's daughters." Eventually, years of caring for the needs of others affected Clyde's physical and emotional health. "His health broke— his nerves followed," said Mary Jane.

His brother lived in Seattle, and Clyde decided it was time to change both his career and his location. For the next 31 years he worked as a finish carpenter for Group Health, finally retiring at age 70. "I planned to retire at 65, but they talked me out of it,"

CLYDE AND MARY JANE, 1945.

he said, and laughed. "They wouldn't let me go!"

His steady faithfulness shone at home, as well. Twenty years ago, when Mary Jane battled colon cancer, Clyde was by her side caring for her. As the cancer spread, Mary Jane said, "The doctor had given me up, but Clyde didn't. He prayed for me and the Lord healed me." He also devotedly cared for her when she suffered a stroke 14 years ago.

As they talked about their seven decades of marriage, they shared their strategy for dealing with disagreements. "We talked our way through it and then didn't bring it up again the next day," said Clyde. Then he reached over and patted his wife's hand, "She's the best wife I could have chosen. I've enjoyed all our years together."

LOVE LESSON

"Really the very best way to have a happy marriage is to put the Lord first in your life."—Clyde Walden

CLYDE AND MARY JANE WALDEN, 2010.
Photo courtesy Dan Pelle, Spokesman Review

Mary Jane Walden died May 4, 2013

CHAPTER 26
THE PILOT AND THE WAVE

WILSON AND CONNIE CONAWAY (RIGHT), 1943; THIS
IS THE ONLY PHOTO OF WILSON IN UNIFORM.

🌿 *Straighten Up and Fly Right*
—NAT KING COLE & IRVING MILLS, 1943

Wilson Conaway didn't care for high school. "It was 1942," he recalled. "The war was on. In Youngstown, Ohio there were a lot of flags waving and I wanted to be a pilot." The one thing he did like about school was a pretty girl named Connie Campbell. "She was running around with my best friend and he introduced us," Wilson said. They went out a few times, but the lure of flying proved stronger than his affection for Connie, and definitely trumped the drudgery of schoolwork.

So he hitchhiked to Cleveland and enrolled in the U.S. Army Air Force. His eyes lit up when he recalled the first aircraft he flew. "I learned to fly in a Stearman. It's a beautiful plane and great for acrobatics!" His instructor was one of the first 25 military pilots in the U.S. "He taught us all the tricks and everything he knew."

While Wilson soared through the skies, Connie and her family moved to California. "We kept in touch by letter," she said. Then she grinned. "I wrote to several male friends—they were all in the service." However, she soon saw her Ohio sweetheart again when Wilson was sent to California for further training, and he enjoyed home-cooked meals with Connie's family. She said, "My mom delighted in feeding the soldiers!"

Wilson had hoped to fly the single-seat P-51 fighters, but instead was assigned to the 92nd Bombardment Group and trained to fly B-17's. "We were replacements," said Wilson. "They were losing so many B-17 pilots." Eventually Wilson, his crew and a brand new plane were sent to England. He completed nine missions over Germany, often flying under heavy fire. He shrugged. "The Germans were mad at us, I guess." The memory of one encounter made him grin. "Our tail gunner got hit in the head. He'd taken off his flak helmet—but it (shrapnel) bounced off his head because he was Greek," Wilson joked. Other memories sadden him. His radio operator, Lynn, was killed on one of those missions. "The night before we left, we all had dinner together, and his wife and little baby came—that was the last time she saw him."

Seventy years later, the death still haunts. "The airplane floor was covered with his blood," he said, rubbing his eyes with the back of his hand. "I tried to get in touch with his wife for many, many years. I wanted to tell Lynn's daughter about her dad." He had his own close encounter with enemy fire. "A piece of shrapnel cut my insulated flight suit at the belt line," he said. The frigid temperatures of high-altitude flight meant that by the time they landed he couldn't move his legs. "It was so cold! They had to lift me out of the cockpit."

After each mission, the pilots had to give a briefing to the officers on the ground. Following the briefings, the crew was rewarded with shots of vodka in little ceramic cups. But after this particular flight, Wilson said, "I didn't have to do my briefing, but I still got my shots!"

While Wilson served his country in Europe, Connie did her part at home. In 1944, she enlisted in the WAVES (the women's section of the US Naval Reserve). She had to provide a letter from her parents to join. "The Navy was very careful with their girls," she said. She explained that one of the reasons she signed up was because, "I was in nurse's training and I decided I didn't like it."

Ironically, her first assignment was at the Long Beach Naval Hospital

CONNIE CAMPBELL, 1944.

where she worked in the Operating Room of the Dependents unit. She laughed. "Gall bladders, tonsillitis—all the fun stuff." She may have been in the military, but like many ladies she was still fashion-conscious. "We were issued such ugly hats!" she recalled. "Everyone wanted the overseas cap because it was cuter."

When the war in Europe ended, Wilson and his men stayed behind, and for the next 18 months they mapped Europe and delivered mail. "We had it real good because our commanding officer was on Eisenhower's staff," he said. "We flew to Rome, Athens, Paris. . . ." And while a few French girls turned his head, none captured his heart.

Both Wilson and Connie were discharged in 1946 and returned to Youngstown. "We found each other again, back in our hometown," Connie said. They picked up where they left off in high school and a few months later, Wilson proposed on the steps outside Connie's apartment building. They married on January 22, 1947.

Despite Wilson's commendable war service, without a high school diploma, he struggled to find work. Their daughter, Dottie, was born in 1948, and a few weeks later they packed up and moved to Whittier, California, where Connie's parents still lived. While looking for a job, Wilson met the Dean of Whittier College. After hearing of his plight, the Dean registered Wilson for college. Wilson recalled, "He said, 'If you can't get a high school diploma, get a college one.'"

And that he did. The young man, who didn't like high school, thrived in college, eventually earning a PhD in education. He landed his first teaching job in Detroit, where he taught 6th grade for three years. "I liked teaching 6th grade," he said. "Because after that they go bananas!"

Another daughter, Connie, joined the family in 1954. They returned to

California and Wilson talked his wife into using her GI Bill to attend college. She received her Bachelor's in English in 1970, and taught English and Home Ec at a local middle school for many years.

"It seems a lot of our married life, one of us was in school," Wilson said. "When you're young you can do anything."

He attributes their shared passion for learning to an equally strong desire for self-improvement. "You sell yourself to society," he said. "I'm the product—I have to improve it." They both retired from teaching in 1990 and finally had time to pursue the hobbies that make them happy. Wilson has been a lifelong painter and his work adorns many walls in their home. "It's just fun," he said.

Connie joined a garden club and soon discovered one new friend had a connection to Wilson. "My friend is German and had been a baby during the war. Her house was bombed and they had to dig her out of the rubble." It turns out Wilson's plane had dropped the bomb that decimated her home. That fact didn't dampen their friendship a bit.

The couple recently returned from an Honor Flight to Washington, DC. Usually, spouses don't go together, but because they are both WWII veterans, they got to take the trip together. "It's something we'll never forget," said Connie. She's also never forgotten how fortunate they've been. Many B-17 pilots never returned. She said, "I've told him many times, 'I'm lucky to have you, honey.'"

And Wilson, who left school and flew around the world, only to find his true love back in his hometown said, "I'll tell you a secret; I love her more today than I ever have."

LOVE LESSON

"Neither of us is perfect. She has little things that rub me wrong, but that's her. She accepts my faults, too."—Wilson Conaway

WILSON AND CONNIE CONAWAY, 2011.
Photo courtesy J. Bart Rayniak, Spokesman Review

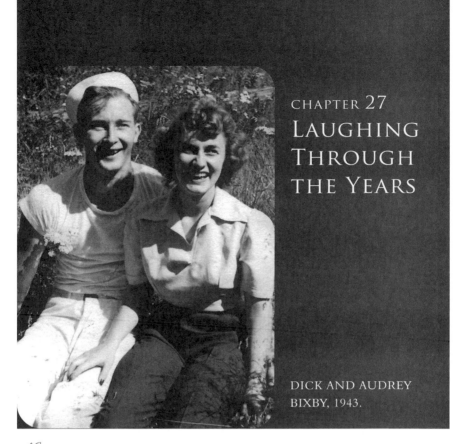

DICK AND AUDREY
BIXBY, 1943.

Is You or Is You Ain't My Baby
— LOUIS JORDAN & BILLY AUSTIN, 1944

Dick and Audrey Bixby met in high school, but Audrey had had her eye on Dick for quite a while. "He was tall and handsome," she recalled. "My girlfriend and I used to drive our bikes around his house, hoping to spot him." By the time friends set them up, Audrey already had plenty of other fellows interested in her. That didn't sit well with Dick. "I walked her home from school and I told her she was going to be my girlfriend or I was going to be long gone," he said.

That declaration motivated Audrey. "I decided I didn't want to let a good one go!" And seven decades later, she's still happy with her choice. In their cozy living room, the couple laughed and teased each other as they recalled their courtship. Once Audrey decided to make Dick her only boyfriend, she never looked back, even when Dick and his family moved away after his graduation.

Audrey, an only child, had grown to love Dick's boisterous family. "I lost my mother at 13," she said. "Dick's mom was my mother from the time we met." Shortly after the Bixbys moved, Audrey's father took a job in Alaska. Sixteen-year-old Audrey didn't want to move to Alaska, so she asked her dad if she could live with her aunt and finish school in Seattle—which just happened to be where her sweetheart and his family lived. Her father agreed and Dick and his mother arrived to help her move. "He came to get me in a Model A Ford with a rumble seat!"

While Audrey loved being included as part of the family, she said, "There were so many things I just didn't get! Like, they'd start water fights and I would run and hide. To this day, I don't like water being thrown at me!"

Dick laughed. "She really didn't get it."

His wife shook her head. "I still don't!"

BIXBY WEDDING,
AUGUST 22, 1942.

Dick served his apprenticeship at a machine shop, and after graduation Audrey found work at a local bank. On December 7, 1941, the couple planned to go ice skating. "We heard about the attack on Pearl Harbor on the radio," Dick recalled. "We didn't quite realize the extent of what it would mean to us."

A new job sent him to Salt Lake City, but the separation from his sweetheart proved too much. "It was understood that we'd marry from the time he told me to get rid of all the other boys," said Audrey. He sent her an engagement ring by mail and after six months in Utah, he decided to hitchhike home. "She was my girl," Dick said. "And I missed her."

There weren't many cars on the road due to gas rationing, and Dick finally arrived in Seattle sporting a painful sunburn. The first thing he said after greeting her was "Let me see the ring!" Unfortunately, Audrey had been so nervous and excited to see him that she inadvertently left her engagement ring on the bathroom sink at work, and she was horri-fied by having to tell him. But true to form, he laughed. Thankfully, the ring was recovered.

They married in her aunt's home on August 22, 1942. "I didn't have enough money to buy both wedding dress and a going away suit, so I got married in a wool suit," Audrey recalled. "It turned out to be the hottest day of the summer!" When Dick signed in at the hotel for their wedding night, he realized he had much to learn about being a married man. "I signed in just myself," he said, laughing. "I told the clerk, 'I'm new at this!'"

As World War II intensified, Dick could have received a deferment be-cause of his work as a machinist. "But I chose to join the Navy," he said. After basic training he was sent to Pasco. "I cleaned barracks and cooked in the galley," he said. But soon his true talents were discovered and he was asked to supervise the aircraft repair facility. "He was in charge of the battery shop" Audrey said. "He did a good job, so they left him alone."

His wife soon joined him, and they rented an upstairs room in an older home. "We lived in that one big room for two years," Audrey recalled. She struggled to learn housekeeping skills. "Dick taught me how to cook after we were married—more or less!" One afternoon she decided to bake a pie to serve guests that evening. "I was rolling the crust out with a milk bottle and I couldn't get it to roll out right. I was crying," she said. So she did what she usually did—she asked her husband for help. He'd been working on their car, and though he washed his hands before rolling out the piecrust, evidently he didn't do a thorough job. "The pie had black flecks in it!" Au-drey said. But they served it to their guests anyway, and laughed while telling them the story. "I still don't like to cook to this day!" she said.

Audrey admits she didn't know anything about babies either, but that didn't stop her from wanting one. "At that time, we thought the war was never going to end and I wanted to start a family, so we did!" In April of 1945, their daughter Nancy arrived. She weighed only 5 pounds and Dick admits to being taken aback by his first glimpse of her, unprepared for how tiny she was. They didn't have much time together, as Dick was soon trans-ferred to San Francisco. After he left, Audrey and the baby moved in with Dick's sister. In October of 1945 he was discharged from the Navy and re-united with his wife and daughter.

The birth of their son, David, in 1948 completed their family. Anxious

DICK AND AUDREY WEARING THE FUR
COAT DICK BOUGHT HER, 1943.

to settle down, they purchased a new home in 1950. "We paid $60 a month," said Audrey. "And we lived there 43 years. Dick added a huge family room and a swimming pool. We had so many parties! We'd roll up the braided rug and dance. Oh, we had such good times!"

After many years of successful employment, Dick became his own boss. His father had started Bixby Machine and Supply and when he wanted to retire, Dick purchased the business from him. Audrey worked with him doing accounting and ordering, and the business thrived. "It was fun," she said. "We made so many friends! We stayed after work and customers would hang out and visit us." She smiled fondly at Dick. "We had good years working together." When they were ready to retire, they sold the business to their son.

Pulling out a photo album, Dick pointed to a picture of an 18-year-old Audrey, "This is who I fell in love with," he said. He choked up—her recent illness had unnerved him. Composing himself, he enumerated her attributes, concluding with the two most important to him. "She's an awfully nice person and she laughs at my jokes!"

Suddenly, the tears he'd fought back filled his eyes, and Audrey reached out and patted his hand. "He's always been proud of me." She leaned forward and confided, "I still dress up for him." As for their long years together, she was matter-of-fact. "In those days that's what you did. You stayed married. You worked at it and you didn't toss it aside if things weren't all smooth sailing."

Her husband cleared his throat. "It's simple," he said, earnestly. "Do what your wife says." Then a huge grin split his face and Audrey rolled her eyes.

"We still have a lot of fun," she said, and added with a grin, "Just not as much." And once again, laughter filled the room.

LOVE LESSON

"Treat your spouse with as much courtesy and politeness as you would a guest in your home."—Audrey Bixby

---

DICK AND AUDREY BIXBY, 2010.

Dick Bixby died September 24, 2013

CHAPTER 28
KEEPING TIME

FLYBOY LOUIS
ANDERSON 1943.

Till the End of Time— BUDDY KAYE & TED MOSSMAN, 1945

Barbara Gilby could scarcely believe her luck when her secret crush walked into her parent's jewelry store in 1945. Tall, handsome Louis Anderson was home on leave from the Army Air Corps and wanted to get his watch fixed.

Louis and Barbara had attended the same high school, but he was a couple of years older than she. When he graduated and left to join the service, Barbara clipped his photo from the yearbook and carried it in her wallet. From her balcony perch, where she worked as an engraver, she watched her father slowly shake his head—the store had been flooded with soldiers home on leave and her dad had a backlog of repairs waiting.

"I didn't have the nerve to come down," Barbara recalled. "After he left, I bawled out my dad for not fixing his watch." She'd hoped Louis would stay in the store a bit longer. If he had, she said, "I felt like I would have worked up the courage to greet him!"

Louis hadn't been around much. "After Pearl Harbor all the guys in high

160

school wanted to be pilots," he said. He was one of them who got his wish, and became a B-17 pilot stationed overseas as part of the 305th Bombardment Group. Their mission was to bomb German railroads, oil refineries and switchyards. A photo shows his flight crew looking impossibly young and irrepressibly confident. Their 22-year-old leader, first pilot Louis Anderson, sits on his haunches in the front row. The photo was snapped as the 10 young men prepared to depart for Chelveston, England. It was May 1944, and the crew of the G-model Flying Fortress eagerly anticipated getting their licks in against the enemy.

Thirty-five missions later, Louis returned home, having lost only one of his original crew. Amazing, because according to Louis, "There was only one mission that we didn't get shot at." He recalled one frightening flight. "We got 300 hits on the right wing alone. On that day we probably had over 1,000 hits." While his crew made it back without a loss, others weren't as fortunate. "That same mission a friend of mine had only six holes in his plane, but he lost his navigator."

Flight crews can be notoriously superstitious. Louis laughs when he recalled the time his crew didn't want to take off until he was the wearing the greasy, stained cap he usually wore. But

LOUIS ANDERSON, 1943.

he, too, realized he could use a little extra protection. He sheepishly admitted, "I carried a New Testament my grandmother gave me on every mission."

One memorable mission left a lasting impression. "Flak went through the floorboard of the cockpit and out the windshield, shattering it," Louis recalled. "I was hit in the back of the leg and a small piece of flak lodged there. It felt like I'd been hit with a baseball bat." And 70 years later, he's pretty sure that souvenir is still stuck somewhere in his leg.

Other memories cause deeper pain. He recounted the first time he and his crew saw a plane shot down. They were flying in a 12-ship squadron, and his friend Clifton Alford, a university music professor, was piloting a nearby aircraft. "They got hit," Louis said. "We didn't see any parachutes. We'd all gone through training together," he paused. "It hit the fellows pretty hard. The romance wore off and they ceased to believe the movies pretty quickly." The first time they saw a plane shot down disturbed them, but nothing prepared them for the horror they witnessed on a subsequent mission.

"A ship in our left wing got hit," Louis said. He and his men watched in dismay as the ball turret gunner fell from his turret and hung suspended by his foot. Many B-17 crew members considered the ball turret the worst position on the aircraft, as the gunner was confined in a sphere fastened to the underside of the plane. Louis cleared his throat. "I had to explain to the fellows that he was no longer with us." After 45 seconds the gunner fell from the aircraft.

"We had quite a bit of difficulty talking the crew into getting back in the plane to fly a mission the next day," he continued. "We had to have several

LOUIS ANDERSON (KNEELING BOTTOM LEFT) AND HIS CREW, 1944.

conferences with the chaplain to explain that the gunner hadn't been hanging there, suffering."

On a different excursion, one of his crew members had a piece of flak go under his helmet and essentially scalp him. "He was really bleeding," Anderson said. They got him safely back to base and after he recovered he was transferred to a different aircraft. Later they found out he'd been killed in action. He was the only member of the original crew who didn't return home.

But on the day Louis entered the jewelry store, his thoughts weren't on the horrors of war—they were on his timepiece and on his mother. He'd re-

LOUIS ANDERSON, 1944.

turned to the states for B-29 training, but his mother's ill health prompted an extended leave. Barbara decided not to keep her crush a secret, and a month after seeing him in the jewelry store, a mutual friend arranged a date for the couple. In fact, she said a number of people encouraged Louis to ask her out. Plus, their brothers were already friends.

Their first date was a romantic success. "We went on a picnic at Crystal Lake," Barbara said. Other dates followed. "I was impressed," said Louis. "She was a beautiful girl." When his leave was up, he rejoined his unit, but returned for another visit just in time for Christmas. Barbara smiled at the memory. "He brought me a bottle of Joy perfume and a box of candy."

On New Year's Eve 1945, the couple headed out to a dance at a local Grange. A winter rainstorm descended with a vengeance. "The rain poured down and the mud flowed," said Barbara. They couldn't get to the Grange, so they sat in Louis's truck and listened to the New Year come in on the radio. And as 1946 arrived, Louis asked Barbara to marry him.

"My dad said he was the first guy I dated that was real man and gentleman," Barbara recalled. Louis bought her a small diamond engagement ring at her father's store. He felt bad about the size of the stone, but he was just getting out of the service and planned to attend college, so there simply wasn't enough cash for a more elaborate ring. Barbara said, "I told him he could get me a bigger diamond for our 25th anniversary." That became a running joke between them. "Every time he missed a birthday or anniversary, the diamond got bigger," she said, and chuckled. "I told him I don't accept apologies—just add it to the cost of the new diamond."

Louis shook his head. "I'm still not sure about the accounting on all that!"

On July 7, 1946, they married. Following World War II, housing for couples was in short supply, so for the first year of their married life they lived in one room in a boarding house.

In 1950, Louis graduated with a degree in education from Washington State University and Barbara gave birth to their daughter. A son later completed the family. Louis served 21 years in the Air Force Reserves and taught high school for 30 years. "When things got boring in class," he said, "the students would get me to talk about my World War II experiences." He laughed. "It was a good strategy."

He also returned to his rural roots. Barbara said, "He grew up on a farm—he was a country boy but I was a city girl." In 1967, the family bought 80 acres in Green Bluff, Washington. "It was part woods and part cleared land," Louis said. "The years up on the farm were the most enjoyable and the least stressful of our lives." His wife, however, wasn't eager to explore farm life. She asked him, "Do you want me to look weathered and old?" He didn't—so she took care of the bookkeeping and sold the plentiful apples and cherries. "But no actual farm work for me!" she said.

They've retained their military ties; their granddaughter is married to Lt. Col. David Banholzer, who until recently served as the pilot of Air Force One. Louis smiled, "Now, he's the only one who'll really listen to my war stories."

The Andersons have stayed busy during their retirement years. Louis is a Master Gardener and Barbara an avid quilter. Every Wednesday morning Louis attends a men's prayer breakfast, but even then, Barbara is on his mind. "He always brings me back a scone," she said.

Having celebrated 68 wedding anniversaries, the couple reflected on their years together. Both share a positive outlook on life. "Stay happy," Barbara said. "Don't waste time being unhappy. Time passes too fast." She said their love for each other has changed over the years. "It's a different kind of love, now. It's truer, deeper and richer." Then she smiled at her husband. "I feel sorry for those who don't grow old together."

And the watch that brought him into the jewelry store more than six decades ago? It was repaired and he still wears it. It's kept on ticking, just like their marriage.

LOVE LESSON
"You can't take back bad words. We've never said one thing we've had to take back."—Barbara Anderson

---

LOUIS AND BARBARA ANDERSON, 2010. *Photo courtesy Ralph Bartholdt*

CHAPTER 29
SECOND LOOK WAS ALL IT TOOK

MELVIN AND
DOROTHY HAYES
WEDDING,
JUNE 18, 1938.

🌿 *I Concentrate On You* — COLE PORTER, 1940

It's not always the first person who catches your eye that matters. Take Melvin Hayes, for example—more than 70 years ago, he spotted his future wife Dorothy at a sledding party. "Somebody else caught my eye first," Melvin recalled. "But then I saw her."

A group of young people had built a big bonfire and spent the day sledding, and after Melvin saw Dorothy, no one else could hold his attention. They went down one run after another until their cheeks were pink and their noses red-tipped, then huddled close together at the fire warming their frozen fingers. As Melvin's hands and feet thawed, so did his heart. Though three and a half years older, he was smitten with the petite Dorothy.

The details of their courtship have grown murky over time. "We didn't 'date,'" he said. "We just saw each other. It was the Depression—we didn't have any money for dating." In fact, Melvin felt grateful to be employed at a motor supply company. It wasn't easy to get the job. "I showed up at eight in the morning and stood there until five in the evening, waiting to see the boss," he said. "Jobs were hard to come by."

Neither of them recalls the specifics of his proposal, either. "We just went together a long time," Melvin said and shrugged. "There wasn't a formal engagement." However, they needed a little help to make it to the altar. Dorothy said, "Our mothers had to go with us to get our marriage license." Melvin was 20 and Dorothy, 17—both too young to marry without parental consent.

On June 18, 1938, the couple married at Dorothy's parents' home. A simple family wedding suited them both. Melvin grinned. "I wouldn't have stood for a flashy wedding!" They settled into a small one-bedroom home— really small. "Tall people couldn't even get in the house without ducking," he said. He earned $20 a week at the motor supply store. "I got a little raise when we got married," he said. A year later when their daughter Marilyn arrived, he got another small raise. "Things were pretty tough," he admitted.

Dorothy didn't mind the lack of money. She'd always loved babies and was thrilled to learn she was expecting again. Unfortunately, she lost the baby, and seventy years later she's still saddened by the memory. "It was difficult," she said.

The birth of their son Melvin (Butch) in 1942, eased her sorrow, and things continued to improve for the family. Shortly after his son's birth, Melvin got a job as an electri-

MELVIN HAYES, 1945.

cian at Hanford Engineer Works in south-central Washington. Established in 1943 as part of the Manhattan Project, Hanford was home to the B Reactor, the first full-scale plutonium production reactor in the world.

He and Dorothy were delighted by the better wages and living quarters, but their delight was short-lived. A draft notice arrived in 1944, so Melvin took the Army physical and waited. The next year another draft notice arrived, so in February 1945, a month after his job at Hanford concluded, Melvin became a soldier. "I was 27-years-old when I left," he said. "It was fun."

Then he shook his head, and chuckled. "Not really! The military was the least of my ambition." From her seat next to him Dorothy grinned and poked his shoulder. "I didn't know you had ANY ambition!" Ignoring her ribbing, he continued. "I was stationed at Fort Lewis when the war with Japan ended and I thought they'd muster me out." But that didn't happen. Instead, in November 1945, he received orders to ship out. "They issued me a down sleeping blanket and a heavy coat," he recalled. With all that gear, he was certain he was headed for Europe. He shook his head, "Then they sent me to Honolulu." Though a trained electrician, he spent his time in the Army as a cook. Glancing at Dorothy, he said, "But I don't cook at home!"

Left: MELVIN HAYES HOME ON LEAVE, WITH SON BUTCH, 1945; *right:* MELVIN HAYES, OCTOBER 1945.

Meanwhile, his wife and kids had moved in with her mother. Soon, Dorothy joined the ranks of working women at the telephone company. "I worked the switchboard from four until midnight. I took the bus to work and they sent me home in a taxi." Because they had two small children, Dorothy petitioned the Red Cross and obtained a hardship discharge for Melvin. "I was home by the first of April," he said.

He worked briefly for the railroad, before returning to his former job at the motor supply store. Two more children joined the family, Shellie in 1950, and Melinda in 1953. Eventually, he and a partner opened their own auto parts store in a neighboring small town. The couple enjoyed the town and the work, but they worried about their aging parents, so in 1964 Melvin took a job with a printing company in their hometown. Dorothy and the kids were happy to be closer to their extended family. For his part, Melvin loved his new job—in fact, he didn't retire until he turned 90. His last pay stub is dated October 20, 2008. "I might still be there if the boss hadn't died on me," he said.

Once the kids were grown and gone, the couple made time for travel, despite Melvin's long hours at work. "I didn't get to go to Hawaii with him the first time," Dorothy said. "But I've been with him several times since!"

Melvin has been an El Katif Shriner since 1959, and they took many trips with fellow Shriners. In fact, he hasn't had much luck retiring from that organization, either. "I've been the treasurer since 1980," he said. Evidently, replacing Melvin is hard to do.

After 72 years of marriage, Dorothy is in no hurry to replace him. "We get along pretty good." Smiling, she willingly confided the secret to their lasting union. "He does what I tell him to!" Melvin loves to garden and she loves to can. "Our 20 ft. by 30 ft. garden is now, 50 by 70, because he kept digging up the lawn," she said, laughing.

Several years ago, the death of their eldest daughter brought a stark reminder of how precious time with loved ones can be. Since that time, each spring the couple and their three remaining children take a trip together— just the five of them. They've enjoyed their trips to Yellowstone and Glacier national parks.

Melvin may not be one for flowery romantic phrases, but his devotion to his wife is clear. He said the best part of a long marriage is the companionship. "It's nice having someone with you all the time—it would be awful to live alone." He's long forgotten the name of the girl who first caught his eye at that sledding party so many years ago. He looked at Dorothy. "Once I saw her, I loved her. She was the one." He cleared his throat. "I don't know what I'd do without her."

LOVE LESSON

"I suppose we've gone to bed mad a few times, but not many."—Melvin Hayes

DOROTHY AND MELVIN HAYES, 2011.
Photo courtesy J. Bart Rayniak, Spokesman Review

Dorothy Hayes died July 2, 2012

CHAPTER 30
THE MARINE AND THE SAILOR

MYRTLE MUELLER, 1943.   WALT POWERS, 1945.

First Class Private Mary Brown — FRANK LOESSER, 1944

Walt Powers never thought he'd fall in love with a Marine, but that's just what happened to him 71 years ago at Marine Corps Air Station Santa Barbara.

Walt was from Texas and had been drafted into the Navy, leaving home on Christmas Day, 1943. He first glimpsed Myrt Mueller at a reception following a change of command ceremony at the base. She was carrying a large decorated cake. "Excuse me," she said. As he stood aside to let her pass, Walt was instantly smitten. "I thought she was the most beautiful Marine I'd even seen!"

Myrt, 21, had been teaching school in Oregon when World War II began. "I had these kids coming in saying, 'My daddy's going to war and I don't know if he's going to be killed.'" She shook her head. "I couldn't take it. I joined the Marines in 1943—I wanted to take care of my students' dads." However, she ended up teaching Marines about airplane maintenance. Walt laughed. "When they found out she didn't know the difference between a spark plug and a generator, they moved her to the dispensary."

She was working as dietician and Walt was a Navy surgical technician when their paths crossed that fateful afternoon. He tracked her down the next day and asked her to go on a bike ride on Sunday. When she told him she'd be happy to but only after she went to church, he knew he'd found a "good" girl. He also knew this because he'd used his job to check her health records. He grinned at the memory. "She was clean!"

Their first date proved unintentionally memorable. In his enthusiasm to get closer to Myrt, Walt crashed his bicycle into hers. Undaunted, he used the opportunity to show off his medical expertise. He took her to the clinic to treat her scrapes. "I used my skill to bandage her arm," he recalled. "And when I got to her knee, I held her leg!"

A bold move indeed, for 1945. Walt worried that she wouldn't go out with him again after the bicycle mishap, but Myrt liked him. "He was a handsome sailor," she said, smiling. One evening they decided to stroll out to the rifle range. "We saw an MP in a jeep coming," recalled Walt. "We worried that we weren't supposed to be there." The couple ran and hid in the latrine. Walt laughed. "It was a very small latrine!"

WALT POWERS, HOME ON LEAVE, 1945.

However, their adventures were suspended when Walt shipped out to Guam, a move that surprised them both since by this time the war was over. Instead of returning to his family in Texas, Walt said, "I became part of the occupation force of Japan and spent time in China, as well." For nine months their only connection came through the mail, and those letters fostered a deep and lasting bond. "We kind of fell in love through letters," Walt said.

Myrt nodded. "I saved all 87 of his letters." She paused and shot him a look. "But he pitched mine." Still, Walt thought of her constantly, especially when he earned enough points to get out of the Navy. "I was so much in love with her; I wanted to see

WALT
POWERS,
GUAM,
1945.

her immediately." Instead of getting discharged back to Texas, he asked the yeoman to print up orders for Oregon, where Myrt had returned to finish college after completing her military service.

During the long journey to Oregon, Walt worried. He wondered, "Is she going to kiss me the same way she did when I left? Has she found another boyfriend?"

When Walt arrived at the train station at 6 AM in May 1946, he found Myrt waiting. "She was wearing a beautiful blue suit and hat, and I gave her a kiss like you do when you're returning from war . . ." He paused and smiled across the room at Myrt. "All doubts were immediately gone." He left for Texas to see his family, but not before securing her promise to become his wife. After he arrived home, he sent her an engagement ring in the mail. "I paid $287 for it at Zales—I still have the receipt."

Myrt had signed a contract to teach school in Eugene, and Walt resumed his education at Baylor University. But he couldn't stand the separation, so he persuaded her to join him at Baylor to get her Master's degree.

WALT POWERS, SAN
FRANCISCO, MAY 1946.

WALT AND MYRT, DECEMBER 1946, THE DAY
THEY GOT THEIR MARRIAGE LICENSE.

By December, their friends were tired of waiting for a wedding. "We were both working at a church, so we asked the pastor to marry us," Walt said. And he did that very day, December 13, 1946. Their friends sprang for a night at a hotel and the next day they got up and went to class. The couple found a room to rent with kitchen privileges, and Myrt earned her master's. When she received a lucrative job offer to teach in McMinnville, Oregon, Walt transferred to Linfield College and they returned to Oregon.

In November 1948, their son Wally was born. The following year Walt graduated with a chemistry degree and looked for a job as a chemist. He couldn't find one, but he did find a job as a substitute teacher and fell in love with education. The family moved to Colorado where Walt earned his master's Degree. Their family grew with the arrival of Jim in 1951, followed by Thomas in 1954. Walt became a high school principal and continued his schooling at night, eventually receiving his doctorate. "I always wanted to be a doctor," he joked.

In 1954, Walt joined the faculty at Eastern Washington University as assistant professor of psychology and education, and taught there for more than 40 years. Myrt resumed her teaching career at a nearby elementary school. Soon they built a home just two blocks from the college campus. Since then the university has grown up around the house.

Walt's expertise in the area of high school counseling brought the family many opportunities. From 1961–1962 they lived in Korea, where Walt worked as an advisor to the minister of education. Their sons relished the adventure of living overseas.

In 1966, the adventure continued when Walt was invited to establish a counselor training program at Keele University in England. "Our boys went to an Edwardian type school and wore suits and ties," Myrt said. The couple has traveled the world both for work and pleasure, from Russia to South Africa and beyond. They currently spend the winter months in Hawaii.

In 2011, Eastern Washington University dedicated the Walter and Myrtle Powers Reading Room in the former Hargraves library, to honor the couple's longstanding commitment to education.

Sadly, they've survived two of their sons. Wally died nine years ago from multiple sclerosis and two years after that, Jim had a sudden heart attack and passed away. The couple feels fortunate that their son Tom and his four children live nearby.

Walt and Myrt Powers have spent their lives educating others, and their 68-year-union offers them yet another educational platform. "We kiss every night and we laugh at each other a lot," said Walt. "She lives in the present, not the future."

Myrt laughed. "Or the past!"

Like many long-married couples, their shared years have blurred the differences they once had. "We're so much alike now that 50% of the time we are thinking about the same thing!" said Myrt. They've learned to give each other their own space and say they rarely argue. Perhaps that's due to a unique strategy. "Every two years, I'm allowed to tell him to shut up," Myrt said. "And I can say it as loudly and clearly as I wish!"

LOVE LESSON
"The smaller the wedding, the longer the marriage!"—Walt Powers

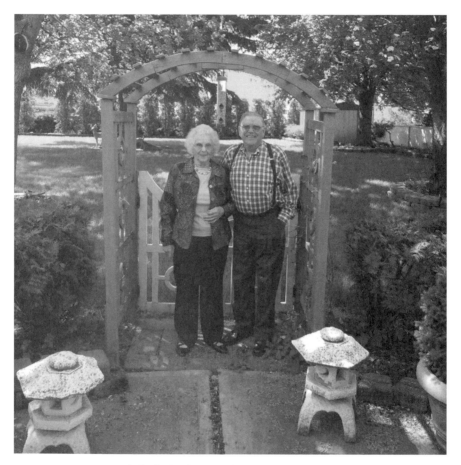

WALT AND MYRT POWERS, 2011.

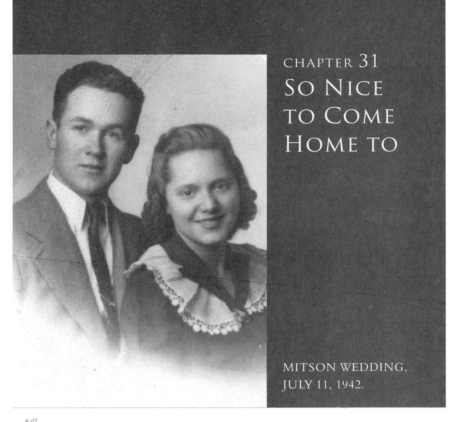

MITSON WEDDING,
JULY 11, 1942.

🌿 *You'd Be So Nice to Come Home to* — COLE PORTER, 1943

On July 11, 1942, Claude (Charlie) Mitson and Mable Harrison, both 17, said "I do," in a tiny church. "I married an older woman," Charlie jested. "She was born in July of 1924 and I was born in September." The two had met at church, but their first impressions of each other weren't promising. Charlie said, "I thought, boy, what a skinny kid that is. I'd hate to be seen with her." Mable wasn't impressed with him either. "He was just another boy," she said. "It took awhile before I realized he might have some prospects."

As part of a small congregation, they were often thrown together, and in this case familiarity did not breed contempt, it bred lasting affection. "We were just really close friends who were going together all the time," Charlie said. "There wasn't an actual proposal, just a mutual agreement." Then he grinned. "She was destined to become my boss!" After graduation he landed a $40 per week job at the newly opened Farragut Naval Station. Charlie said, "I decided I could afford to get married."

17-YEAR-OLD MABLE
HARRISON MITSON.

In June 1943, he received a draft no-tice. He recalled the words with a smile: "Your friends and neighbors have selected you to represent them on the field of battle . . ." Charlie said goodbye to Mable and their infant son, Larry, and left to serve his country. He'd always wanted to be a pilot. "I had a cousin who was a lady pilot. She was my inspiration and ideal." However, his recruiter convinced him the fastest way to flight school was to enlist as a par-atrooper. "That turned out to be another recruiting story," he said with a wry grin. "I spent the entire war as a paratrooper in Europe."

He jumped into Southern France and fought his way through France and Italy, eventually fighting near Anzio and in the Battle of the Bulge. "It was pretty chaotic," Charlie said. "A lot of peo-ple shooting in all directions, with German and American tanks. . . ."

CHARLIE (LEFT) AND A
FRIEND, FRANCE, 1945.

CHARLIE MITSON,
FRANCE, 1945.

Mable said, "I remember him telling me 'You just had to go over the dead and dying and keep moving.'" In one skirmish he followed his lieutenant, crawling along a ridge under heavy German mortar fire. "He was hit and killed instantly, but it didn't touch me," said Charlie.

He counts himself lucky. His only injury came from a piece of shrapnel that struck his leg. He shrugged. "I didn't even know I was hit, 'til someone said, 'you're bleeding!' They put a bandage on it and I just kept going."

Back at home, Mable kept busy. She briefly waitressed at a local café, but felt the sailors from the nearby naval station were a bit too friendly. A job as a stock records clerk at the Naval Supply Depot suited her better.

Charlie spent six months in Berlin and finally, in December 1945, returned home. "I met him at the train station," recalled Mable. "It had been about a year and a half since I'd seen him—I wondered if I'd recognize him." She beamed at the memory. "But I did. Oh, I did!" Likewise, her husband remembers his first glimpse of her after their long separation. "I saw her standing on the staircase." Though the station must have bustled with travelers, Charlie said, "As I remember, she was the only one there."

Though the war was over, Charlie still dreamed of flying. He used the G.I. Bill to take flight instruction, and after earning his commercial pilot's license he became a flight instructor.

A second son joined the family in 1947. "Mable and the boys used to come out and watch me teach students to fly at the airfield."

In 1948, Charlie discovered that the Air Force was looking for cadets and had briefly opened the program to married men. With his wife's blessing, he signed up. "He loved flying," Mable said. "And I was happy with whatever he liked to do. It opened up a world of excitement and travel." Charlie graduated as a second lieutenant in 1950 and spent the next 30 years as an Air Force fighter pilot. He had the thrill of being part of the first squadron to land on an aircraft carrier.

Meanwhile, his wife had her own set of adventures moving her family 22 times in 29 years. "Travelling with the little boys was exciting and terrifying," said Mable, laughing. "But you go where they tell you to go." And for Charlie that meant Korea. "I flew F-86 Sabres in Korea. That was the finest aircraft the Air Force ever had. "

During his 100 missions over the course of the war, Charlie shot down and was credited for 2-1/2 MiG's (Russian-made fighter jets). Fortunately,

CHARLIE MITSON AS A NEWLY
MINTED PILOT, 1950.

he returned home unscathed. "The only way you can get along in that kind of business is to feel that you're invincible," he said. Like most pilots he had his talismans—a piece of scripture torn from his mother's Bible and a silver dollar. "I carried them with me through Korea and Vietnam."

In 1952, Mable gave birth to their third son and still managed to keep up with the constant relocations. She said, "I followed him everywhere." Eventually, two daughters completed the busy family. While stationed in the Mediterranean, Charlie paid a visit to southern France. He said, "I even found an old foxhole I'd dug 10 years earlier and an old German field kitchen." Thirty years later he'd return again to find the foxhole still there.

All too soon, America was at war again. Charlie flew 100 missions over Vietnam. He shook his head. "I was a 42-year-old grandpa flying fighters into the most heavily defended area in the world." And the nature of battle had changed. "We had to deal with a lot of anti-aircraft fire," he said. Surface-to-air missiles took a devastating toll. "We lost aircraft almost every day. I went over as a flight leader, but we kept losing people. We eventually lost our squadron commander."

Charlie took his place and was promoted to Lieutenant Colonel. And that lucky silver dollar? When he returned from Vietnam he gave it to his son David, who was just leaving for combat. David flew 240 missions in Vietnam, and also returned home safely—the Mitson luck held. But Charlie finally had enough adventure. He retired from the Air Force as a colonel at age 54. After working for six years as a realtor, he officially retired from working life: kind of.

"I can't keep up with him," Mable said. Since 1988, Charlie has volunteered with the local police department and been active in various service organizations.

For those who want to know the secret to a long and happy marriage, the Mitsons offered these words of wisdom. "Make sure you have a good solid friendship before you get married," said Charlie. "We've had a very loving 72 years together."

Mable smiled at her husband and said, "I've always had a positive attitude. Wherever he was I always knew he was coming home."

LOVE LESSON
"You've got to trust each other and not doubt."—Mable Mitson

CHARLIE AND MABLE MITSON, 2010.
Photo courtesy Jesse Tinsley, Spokesman Review

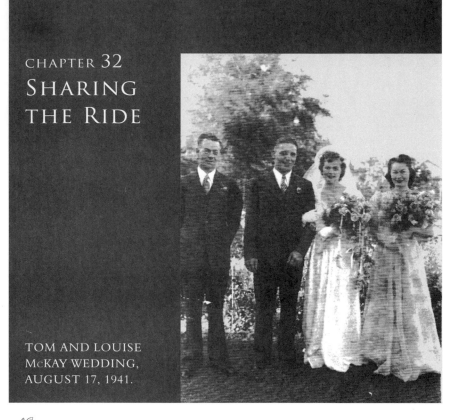

CHAPTER 32
SHARING
THE RIDE

TOM AND LOUISE
McKAY WEDDING,
AUGUST 17, 1941.

🎵 *Down the Road a Piece* — DON RAYE, 1940

C ash-strapped college students often look for ways to stretch their
meager resources. Tom McKay did. In 1940, while attending Eastern Washington College of Education (now Eastern Washington
University) he gave rides to several students to help defray his gas costs. "I
had to pay eighteen cents a gallon," he recalled.

Thriftiness was second nature to him. He'd paid for college and helped
support his family during the Depression by picking huckleberries in the
mountains of Montana. He picked the berries by beating the bushes into a
large shallow canvas container. Often he would pick 35 gallons a day, and
along with his older brother would sell the berries to various stores.

One of the students that joined him on his daily commute was a pretty
girl named Louise Strosnider. She described their first meeting. "Tom
stopped by my house with a friend. These two brash young men were brag-
ging about everything." She smiled. "They were so cute!" But Tom, 21, especially interested her. They got to know each other during their drives to

and from college. "We became friends," said Louise. "We got friendlier and friendlier."

They both chuckled. Tom added, "Actually, she had a boyfriend. I told her, 'He's just a boy and I'm a man.'" That boyfriend didn't last long. "She told me she got rid of him," he said, grinning across the table at Louise.

When the college advertised a Tolo Dance (a girl-ask-boy dance), Louise seized the opportunity and asked Tom to be her date. "We had to dress up like characters from comic strips," she said. "Tom was Chief Wahoo and I was the Indian maiden Minnehaha." Their courtship continued with long walks around the campus. Finally, one day Tom said, "Well. When do you want to get married?"

They settled on a date and Tom decided he'd better quit school, get a job and build a house for his bride. Building materials were in short supply, but he and his dad and brother found an old hotel in a nearby town that was scheduled for demolition. "We salvaged the boards, lumber and even the nails," he said. He took a job as a locomotive fireman for Northern Pacific Railroad and worked on the house every chance he got. Louise helped too. "She straightened the nails," he said.

They married on August 17, 1941. Four months later, Louise was at her parent's grocery store when she heard the news of the Japanese attack on Pearl Harbor. "We were all in shock," she said. She feared that Tom would soon be drafted, but because he worked for the railroad, he received a deferment. And he continued to receive deferments for three years. Louise said, "I was starting to feel maternal. I said, 'Why don't we have a baby?'"

Their daughter, Colleen, arrived February 14, 1944. Six months later, Tom received his draft notice—there would be no more deferments. "He called me from the roadhouse and I knew," Louise recalled. "I said, 'Hello, soldier.'" Her eyes clouded at the memory. Looking out in the autumn sunshine, she shook her head. "I felt just sick."

When Tom left for basic training, Louise and the baby went to stay at her parent's farm. She kept busy with her daughter and drove her dad's big tractor during harvest. Tom called her every Sunday from Camp Roberts in California. One Sunday after harvest, Louise told him, "I'm coming down to see you."

He replied, "No way! This is no place for a woman."

She and the baby came anyway, arriving in a 1937 Cadillac. Louise said,

Left: TOM, LOUISE AND DAUGHTER COLLEEN,
CAMP ROBERTS, 1944; *right:* TOM MCKAY, 1944.

"I thought if he's going to war and getting killed, I'm going to spend as much time with him as possible." They had two months together before Tom shipped out.

When asked what job he was trained for in the Army, Louise promptly answered for him. "Shooting people." The grim reality was that Tom's company, like many others, were replacement troops—bodies to replace the growing list of U.S. casualties.

In April of 1945, Tom and other members of the 32nd Infantry, 7th Division, watched the invasion of Okinawa from a ship in the harbor. Several days later, he and his unit were packed into landing craft and deposited on a beachhead in the dead of night. He said, "For the next two months it was just a matter of slogging away. The Jap soldiers were extremely brave. They weren't easy to take. They wouldn't give up—we just had more people and supplies."

One afternoon Tom and his interpreter got separated from their company. Tom said, "All at once a young Okinawan woman came from a cave. The interpreter said she wanted to know if we could take her family to a safer area. I said sure."

It turned out her family consisted of approximately 30 people who spilled out from the cave. One was a wounded Okinawan soldier, still wearing his uniform pants, carried by his father. Tom's eyes filled with tears at the memory. "His father wouldn't put him down—he carried him all the way off the island." It was dark by the time they finally rejoined their company. "They thought I'd been killed," Tom said. "But they were more worried about my interpreter—he was more valuable."

The battle for Okinawa was brutal and Tom didn't escape unscathed. He recalled, "One afternoon, we crested a hill and they let loose and killed both point men and shot the medics. It was kill or be killed. I had four hand grenades and I was big and strong. I could throw them farther than they could." He hunkered in against a rock and exchanged fire with the enemy. "It went on all morning long. I got five or six guys." Finally, he felt a bullet tear through his right shoulder. It went out through the back of his arm, shattering his shoulder. "It didn't even knock me down," said Tom. "I said, 'Well. They got me.'"

Certain he was going to die, he staggered to a clump of bushes. "I didn't die right then, so I drank a couple canteens of water and ate a handful of hard candy." Then he got up, and though wounded, killed two more enemy soldiers and led his men on an attack that caused the enemy to retreat. He returned to his company with valuable information that enabled the troops to reach their objective with a minimum of casualties.

For his heroic efforts he received a Bronze Star and a Purple Heart.

Many men died that day and somehow a newspaper thought Tom had been one of them. Thankfully, the first thing he'd done while recuperating from his injury was to write his wife a letter. He had to use his left hand, but she could make out his scrawl and still treasures that letter. She shrugged. "I read in the paper that he'd been killed, but I'd already heard from him."

In that letter he wrote, "If wishing would   TOM MCKAY, 1944.

help, I'd be with you now." And he signed it, "Yours always and always." When he returned home from the service he went to the railroad to see if he could get his old job back. "They took one look at me and said, 'You're all done firing.'"

Tom still bears the physical scars of that battle and can no longer raise his right arm above his head. The emotional scars took time to heal, as well. He was haunted by what he'd seen, heard and done. But unlike many World War II soldiers, he talked about his experiences with his wife. "He'd say, 'Oh, the men I've killed . . . ." she recalled. "And he finally got so he didn't talk about it as much."

He and Louise sold everything they had and bought 920-acre ranch with her parents. Tom felt like farm work would be the best rehabilitation for his shoulder. They enjoyed the work and the beautiful location. Their family grew with the birth of Nancy in 1946 and Tom in 1949.

In the ensuing years Tom added teacher to his resume. He taught 7th and 8th grade and then taught high school for six years. Their daughter Christie was born in 1951. Not long after, Tom decided to finish the education that marriage had interrupted. The family moved to Cheney, Washington and lived there for three years, while he earned his Master's Degree. Louise too, finished her education and earned her BA in Education in 1958.

Tom and Louise taught school. They held on to their ranch property and he built a log cabin on it. "The kids loved it," said Louise. After retiring in 1979, he got busy fulfilling a promise he'd made to Louise. "I promised I'd build her a big new house, and I did." Using a one-man sawmill, he built his bride a beautiful two-story home. They enjoyed nightly Scrabble matches and Louise often read aloud to him, so they could enjoy books together.

When they celebrated their 70th anniversary, Louise wore her wedding dress for the occasion. "Well, I squeezed into it," she said. She said their marriage has been made easier thanks to Tom's easygoing ways. "He just came with a sweet disposition."

Much has changed in their seven decades together. They weathered the loss of their daughter Christie, who died in a car accident in 1991. Louise said, "There's nothing like losing a child."

Their five grandchildren give them joy and Tom said their marriage has been built on mutual respect and shared values. "The kids can't believe we never fight, but after the war I felt like I was living on borrowed time." He didn't want to waste precious moments squabbling with the love of his life. It's been many years since the couple carpooled together on their way to college, but Tom smiled at Louise and said, "She's still my sweetheart."

LOVE LESSON

"We just don't quarrel and we make all our decisions together."—Louise McKay

---

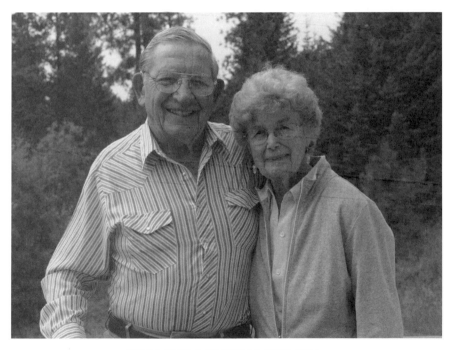

TOM AND LOUISE McKAY, 2011.
Photo courtesy J. Bart Rayniak, Spokesman Review

Tom McKay died July 1, 2013

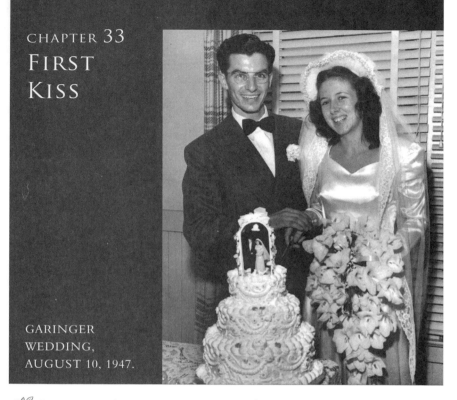

CHAPTER 33
FIRST KISS

GARINGER
WEDDING,
AUGUST 10, 1947.

🌿 *Besame Mucho* — CONSUELO VELÁZQUEZ, 1940

L ots of sweethearts celebrate Valentine's Day, but for David Garinger, February 14 is unforgettable. That's because on that date in 1947, he kissed his future wife for the first time.

They'd gone out on a double date and were sitting in a Hudson coupe, listening to the radio. "I had my arm around Zelma, sitting close. I smelled her sweetness. Her dark shining hair and sparkling blue eyes worked their magic on me. Our lips met for the very first time . . . it seemed so right. Truly she was my Valentine." David penned that flowery description of their first kiss 52 years after that date. He added a PS: "She's still my Valentine."

And now after more than six decades of marriage, it still seems right. Zelma smiled as he read his prose. She was just 16 when they met at Los Angeles Pacific College. David was instantly smitten with the young beauty, but Zelma said, "I didn't want to go out with him. He was too old!" In fact she told her father, "Some old Marine wants to date me."

He'd just turned 23.

David had left school at 17 and learned the construction trade before enlisting in the Marine Corps in 1942. After stateside duty, he shipped out from Camp Pendleton to the South Pacific where he spent 38 months—most of it on Banica Island. His duties weren't too onerous (he was a driver for a general), but while living in tents and Quonset huts, he dreamed of building a real home and a family.

Zelma knew of David before they met because her best friend had dated him for awhile—in fact that friend wrote to him the entire time he was overseas. But that relationship came to naught and once David met Zelma, he knew exactly what and who he wanted.

His war service forced him to grow up quickly, and with that maturity came patience. That "old Marine" also just happened to know a thing or two about persistence, and after some convincing, Zelma agreed to be his date for the college Christmas banquet in December 1946. By August 10, 1947, she was his wife. Wedding photos show a beaming couple who are often caught laughing. "The ring bearer stepped on my floor-length veil," Zelma said. Then she giggled. "It came right off!"

DAVID GARINGER, 1945.

They spent their honeymoon in a cabin at Big Bear Lake. They boated, bicycled and fished. Maybe some new brides wouldn't want to bait hooks on their honeymoon, but Zelma said, "I grew up fishing with my dad."

Too David's dismay, their first home was a tiny Quonset hut courtesy of student housing for veterans. Zelma didn't mind it a bit. "It was like playing house!" Though she continued to take some college classes, it wasn't long before her maternal instinct kicked in. "We were in veterans' housing," she recalled. "Everyone was having babies."

In 1949, the Garingers welcomed the first of their four children. The

DAVID GARINGER,
HAWAII, 1946.

following years were eventful and filled with many moves. David continued his education at Seattle Pacific University, graduating in 1951. He worked as a pastor, a carpenter and general contractor, and the family moved wherever his work took him. "It's amazing looking back," said Zelma. "Life was so busy. We must have had hard times; it just doesn't seem that way to me."

Her love of the outdoors served her well when their children were young. "We always camped," Zelma said. "When the kids were little we used a station wagon and we all slept outside. Eventually, we graduated to a camper and then a trailer."

After the birth of their fourth child in 1961, Zelma returned to college and graduated with a teaching degree. "After the children left, life was really different," she admitted. Still, the couple adjusted to their new lives. Zelma taught elementary school for 30 years and David didn't retire until he was 75.

When the couple moved from California to Washington to be near their youngest child, they didn't settle into a retirement community. Instead, they chose a home in a bustling neighborhood filled with young families. They enjoy their neighbors and having children around them. The Garingers' active lifestyle has continued in their retirement years. "We went on an Alaskan cruise for our 50th anniversary," Zelma said. "From then on we just kept going. We really got the bug." The couple has visited 31 countries in the past 10 years.

Like many married folks, the Garingers admit to being opposites. "He's usually positive and I'm a worrier," Zelma said. When asked about their favorite travel adventure, David said, "I think China was our most exciting trip." However, his wife chose Norway. "We took a train trip through the mountains," she said. "It was so beautiful."

Zelma describes her husband as extroverted and vigorous. "He still has excess energy," she said, laughing. "I can still shovel snow when my neighbors will let me," David said. Zelma is more sedate and enjoys quiet hobbies like quilting and reading, but over the years they've learned the necessary skills of compromise and negotiation. "It helps to have our own space," said Zelma. She has her quilting room on one side of their home, and her husband has his office on the other. He writes, paints in oil, and keeps busy helping at a nearby church camp.

David wishes couples would heed the wisdom of long-married folks. Sitting close to Zelma he patted her knee and sighed. "Young people today give up too quickly," he said. While differences can cause conflict, he's grown to appreciate his wife's savvy ways. "She's always been so sensible about money," he said. "Couples need to talk about money."

Pragmatism aside, he hasn't lost his romantic streak. Each morning he brings his wife a cup of coffee in bed. "He likes to celebrate things," Zelma said. "On my birthday last week he brought my coffee and a little piece of birthday cake with a candle lit." David smiled at his bride. "She's always busy and upbeat. She just keeps going."

Sixty plus years after that first Valentine's kiss, their advice to others lovers is straightforward. "It's give and take," David said. "You decide you want to be together and cooperate with each other."

"Don't expect it to be perfect," said Zelma. "Love is a decision."

LOVE LESSON

"Just keep getting along. It's okay to have differences of opinion—you don't always have to agree."—David Garinger

DAVID AND ZELMA GARINGER, 2008.
Photo courtesy Christopher Anderson, Spokesman Review

David Garinger died June 5, 2014

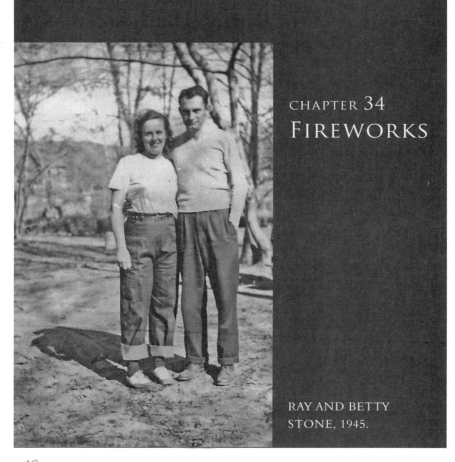

CHAPTER 34
FIREWORKS

RAY AND BETTY
STONE, 1945.

🎵 *The Carousel Waltz*— RICHARD RODGERS, 1945

R ay Stone and Betty Boyle met for the first time on the Fourth of
July, 1936—however, fireworks did not immediately ensue.
Twelve-year-old Betty was taking a spin on the merry-go-round
when Ray, 13, approached. "He said, 'Can I ride with you, sister?'" Betty
recalled. "I said, 'I'm not your sister.'" And that was that.

The two grew up in towns just eight miles apart; Betty in Winchester,
Idaho and Ray in Craigmont. "In small towns like that you just look around
for the girls and find the one you like and go for it," said Ray. So when he
came across Betty again when he was a sophomore in high school, he asked
her out. However, she lived with her aunt and uncle and they refused to let
her date until she was 16. So Ray waited.

The two began dating shortly after Betty's birthday. "Ray used to come
over on Sundays and have dinner with us," Betty said. "I got a free dinner
that way," Ray explained. But he did his part—he'd bring the meat for the
meal after charging to his family's account at the local grocery store.

Ray started drumming while in high school and soon had a regular gig. "I drummed with the band on Saturday nights and earned $8," he recalled. "Then the next day I'd go out and spend it all on Betty."

After graduation, Ray attended college in Lewiston, but the events of December 7, 1941 interrupted his education. "We were having Sunday dinner when we heard about the attack on Pearl Harbor," Betty said. Ray immediately wanted to do his part. "I tried to join the RAF, but I couldn't get across the border."

Instead, he enlisted in the Army and was assigned to the 82nd Airborne Division, and sent to Texas for training. Betty, still a senior in high school, missed her sweetheart, but he faithfully wrote to her. One letter in particular stands out. Betty said, "Just before I graduated Ray wrote me a letter, asking me to come to Texas and marry him. I hid that letter in my Bible."

Her mother opposed the marriage, so Betty enrolled at the University of Idaho. But Ray kept writing and Betty continued to respond. As the war

Left: BETTY BOYLE AT THE UNIVERSITY OF IDAHO, 1944; *right:* RAY STONE, FT. BENNING, 1943. ON THE BACK OF THE PHOTO RAY WROTE, "FORCED SMILE. NOT HAPPY."

efforts intensified, Betty moved to Portland where she worked as a welder in the shipyards. There another proposal from Ray reached her. This time he also sent a ring in the mail, and this time, Betty accepted. She traveled by train to San Angelo, Texas. The train was packed with troops, so Betty spent most of the journey sitting on the floor of the restroom.

On July 8, 1944, the couple exchanged vows in a small Presbyterian church. Ray had reserved a room at the Cactus Hotel. "My aunt and uncle gave us $25 for a wedding photo, but we spent it on the hotel and a steak dinner for the wedding party of four," said Betty. She found a room to rent for $10 per month. "If my husband came for the weekend, the landlady charged an extra dollar."

One month later, Ray was sent overseas.

He fought in three campaigns including the Battle of the Bulge. And always Betty was on his mind. In a V-Mail sent from Belgium during that battle, Ray wrote: "I think about you always Betty. The feeling and the love I have for you has grown into something much deeper than small talk & sayings."

The vagaries of fate haunted him. "I'm feeling plenty lucky," he wrote, "because some of my former friends weren't so lucky." The horrors of war became most apparent to the young paratrooper when he and his company liberated Camp Wobbelin in Nazi Germany. He and his fellow troopers found 1,000 dead—mostly Jews—and another 3,000 dying prisoners in the compound, a way station for men, women and children on their way to Auschwitz or Bergen-Belsen.

Years later in a newspaper interview, he remembered that day as, "The most fearsome, depressing, traumatic experience of my life." As Ray recalled that difficult time, he briefly gazed out of their living room window,

RAY STONE, PARATROOPER, 1944.

V-MAIL TO BETTY, FROM BELGIUM, 1945.

with its stunning lake view. He shrugged, shook his head and said, "It was bad, but what the hell."

It was bad alright. Betty said, "He had terrible nightmares. He'd wake up screaming. He'd seen his friends killed and he wondered why he was spared." While her husband was fighting his way across Germany, Betty had returned to Winchester and began teaching school. "I was only 20," she said. "But I was teaching band to some of the kids I had been in band with!"

Finally, in February 1946, after marching in the historic Victory parade in New York City, Ray returned home. He might have stayed in the military longer, but he said, "I was a troublemaker—I didn't keep my mouth shut."

They bought a new house for $1,200 and Ray went to work at the lumber mill.

However, he didn't stay there long. Thanks to the GI Bill, Ray was able to complete the education the war had interrupted. He earned a B.A. from Whitworth University in 1951, and a master's in education the following year. Betty continued her education as well and received a degree in counseling from Whitworth. They both taught in Coeur d'Alene public schools, but soon Ray began a long career at North Idaho College. Eventually, he was appointed dean.

In 1957, Betty spotted a little boy with blond curly hair on the school playground. Something about the child captivated her. "He looked angelic," she recalled. "But he wasn't." After talking with the child's teacher she discovered that eight-year-old Daniel was a troubled little boy. He'd already lived in eight homes in the past year and was soon to be sent to an orphanage. Betty couldn't have that. She and Ray adopted their only child and brought him home. Sadly, Daniel died in 2001.

Ray served eight years as a city councilman and later served two terms as mayor of Coeur d'Alene from 1985 to 1994. During his tenure, the neo-Nazi, Aryan Nations organization did its best to wreak havoc in North Idaho. "It was a scary time. They'd harass by phone," Betty said. "They'd call us and play that song, 'You're no good, you're no good, baby you're no good.'" She wearied of the nightly interruptions. "I wanted to get an unlisted number but Ray said 'no.'"

"I wasn't afraid of them," he said. His fearlessness and staunch defense of human rights didn't go unnoticed. In 1987, Stone and others accepted the Raoul Wallenberg Award, presented to the city for its human rights work.

That wasn't the only honor he received. In 1988, council members of the new U.S. Holocaust Museum in Washington, D.C., summoned Stone to the nation's capital to award him the Eisenhower Liberation Medal for his part in the liberation of Wobbelin and because of Coeur d'Alene's stand for human rights. Meanwhile at home, he didn't quite get the hang of keeping the peace. Betty didn't mind that a bit. She, better than anyone, understood that buried beneath that crusty demeanor laid a tender heart.

She acknowledged the couple has often clashed over the years. "I have very different philosophies of life," Betty said.

"She's more politically conservative," added her husband.

His musical career picked up steam in his retirement years. He drums for the Ray Stone Swing Band and the group is always in demand. While Betty enjoys music, their hobbies haven't always meshed. Ray mentioned he enjoys golf, which prompted Betty to laugh and say, "I was a very good golf widow." She did attempt to learn the game and took a few lessons, but Ray wasn't impressed with her grip and told her so. She didn't appreciate his comments.

"She said, 'I'm going home,'" Ray recalled. "I said, 'You can't! We've still got a lot of balls in the bucket.'"

"Watch me," she replied and walked home.

Betty raised her eyebrows and smiled. "We quarrel a lot."

Her husband agreed. "She's bossy," he said.

"I'm always telling him how to improve himself," explained Betty. "I try to tell him to be nice and sometimes, he will." But Ray Stone has always spoken his mind. However feisty their disagreements, Ray said what matters most is this: "In the final analysis we love each other. She's been the best person I could have chosen for my kind of lifestyle. Everything I've wanted to do in life, Betty has supported."

And in the summer when the Stones celebrate their next anniversary they plan to take a spin on a carrousel. Betty said, "This time I'll let him ride with me."

LOVE LESSON

"The secret to a good marriage is acceptance. I accept her how she is, not what I'd like her to be."—Ray Stone

RAY AND BETTY STONE, 2010. *Photo courtesy Ralph Bartholdt*

Ray Stone died June 17, 2013

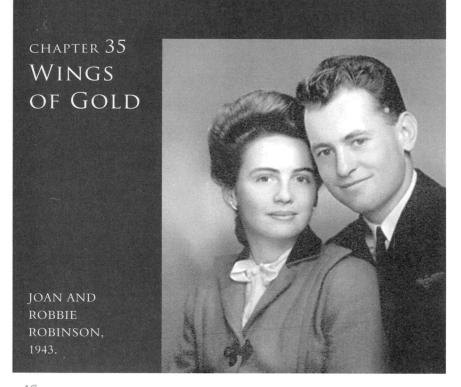

CHAPTER 35

WINGS
OF GOLD

JOAN AND
ROBBIE
ROBINSON,
1943.

🌿 *Coming in on a Wing and a Prayer*
— HAROLD ADAMSON & JIMMY McHUGH, 1943

Meeting at a high school debate club in Long Beach, California, didn't lead to an argument for Joan and F. Willard (Robbie) Robinson—instead it led to a lifetime of love. Robbie, then a senior, served as moderator at a debate Joan participated in. "She was a bright girl and very beautiful," he recalled. "She still is!"

Though he drove her home after the debate, he didn't ask her out. "He was very careful about not dating just one girl," Joan said. Which is a nice way of saying Robbie was quite popular with the ladies.

Robbie laughed. "But now, she's my only girl!" In addition, his mind was on other things at that time—mainly college. He attended the University of Southern California for two years, before his yearning for adventure drew him to the University of Alaska in 1939. While there, he was recruited by the Civil Aeronautics Authority. "I was the first military-trained pilot in the territory of Alaska," he said. He returned to Long Beach in 1940 to complete his studies, but kept his pilot's license current by renting a Piper Club on the weekends. His skills would soon come in handy in ways he'd never imagined.

On December 7, 1941, the Japanese bombed Pearl Harbor. On December 8, Robbie applied for Navy flight training. One month before graduation, he received orders to report to Corpus Christie, Texas. USC agreed to let him skip his finals. Though unable to attend his college graduation ceremony, he was awarded a degree in economics.

Off to Texas he went. After training in a Stearman biplane, he moved on to bigger things. "I flew the Avenger," Robbie said. "That was a hell of an airplane—huge and gorgeous, but terrible to fly. It was uh, pretty adventurous."

To say the least. Landing these torpedo bombers on aircraft carriers in the dead of night was fraught with danger. "The day I qualified, three pilots in my class were killed." Sadly, the casualty list included his friend Bob Koonze, whose plane stalled directly in front of Robbie on Koonze's final landing approach. "He'd only been married 29 days," said Robbie. He paused. His voice caught. "I had to tell his wife." That experience shook him and made him think of Joan. He hadn't seen her for two years, but he hadn't forgotten her. "I knew I cared for her," he said. "But I was in no position to get married."

The loss of his best friend showed him how life can change in a heartbeat. On the train ride home for leave, he felt eager to find Joan. "I get these little visions of things I should do," he said.

His mother told him Joan was working at a bank in Long Beach.

"He walked into the bank and surprised me," recalled Joan. "I said, 'Robbie! What are you doing here?'" She hadn't forgotten about him, either. "He took me out to dinner that night and on the way home he said he had something he wanted to ask me."

ROBBIE ROBINSON, NAVAL AVIATOR.

Though they didn't know each other well, Robbie plunged ahead. He looked into Joan's eyes and said, "I'm going to ask you a very important question, but I don't want you to answer now. In three days, I'll call you from Seattle. You can give me your answer then."

"What's the question?" she asked.

"Will you marry me?"

Stunned, she sat quiet for the rest of the ride home.

After waiting three days, Robbie called.

Joan had her answer ready. "Yes," she said. "Yes, I'll marry you."

Seventy years after that fateful phone call, Joan explained, "I've never been more confident of anything in my life—I just *knew* him. Even though we hadn't had many dates, I really cared a lot for him."

The next week he sent her a train ticket to Seattle. She'd never been away from home.

"That took a lot of nerve," Robbie said.

She arrived on March 1, 1943 and three days later, they married.

The wedding took place at a Methodist church at the University of Seattle. "We got married in the choir loft, and Robbie's whole squadron came."

ROBBIE ROBINSON,
IN DRESS UNIFORM.

Joan laughed. "In fact, I was the only woman at the wedding except for the organist!"

Her husband grinned. "It was an amazing thing, really."

They honeymooned during their drive to California, where Robbie was scheduled to report for duty. "We had a whole year together, but I lived at 13 different addresses during that year," said Joan. Finding accommodations for married military couples proved difficult at best, but she didn't complain about the frequent moves. She felt blessed to be with her husband.

Still, Robbie said, "It was hard on her. She was alone a lot." His wife agreed the loneliness was difficult, but she said, "It's just part of growing up."

In January 1944, Robbie kissed Joan goodbye and shipped out to Pearl Harbor with his torpedo squadron, assigned to bomb the Japanese strongholds in the Marshall Islands. In March 1944 Robbie took off from his ship, the USS *Manila Bay,* with a full payload of bombs. The crew didn't spot any enemy activity and at dusk they headed back to the ship.

Robbie related what happened next in his book, *Navy Wings of Gold.* The weight of the explosives made an already tricky landing more difficult, and as they made their approach, Robbie knew they were in trouble. "Without warning the plane lurched and trembled. Like a goose hit in the wing by a volley of shot, we plummeted into the Pacific with terrifying finality."

The plane smashed into the water, shattering on impact. Cascades of water tossed him about like limp seaweed. Blown from the aircraft and barely conscious, he tripped the release on one side of his May West lifejacket, and it partially inflated, supporting his head.

He was plucked from the sea by the crew of a nearby destroyer. Later that night he learned that his radioman, George Driesback Jr., and his gunner, Harold Eckert, had been killed on impact. "They never had a chance," he said. "They were in the belly of the plane." Robbie's right leg was ripped open and shrapnel embedded in the base of his spine. His face was gashed and his body covered with contusions and lacerations. But none of his injuries compared to the pain and heartache of losing his friends, just 19 and 22 at the time. For years afterward, he'd awake from nightmares about the crash, drenched in sweat and shaking from the horror of the scenes that played in an endless loop in his head, even in his sleep. The nightmares have faded over time, but the pain of losing his friends is still raw.

Back in California, Joan experienced her own heartache. The doorbell rang at her parents' home. A delivery boy handed her a telegram that read: "The Navy Department regrets to inform you that your husband Lieutenant Junior Grade Franklin Willard Robinson Jr. as been seriously injured in a plane crash while in action in the performance of his duty and in the service of his country. . . ."

Weeks stretched into months. "I didn't hear a word," she said. "I was terrified, but still I was confident that he would come back." Finally, a thoughtful nurse sent Joan a note, informing her that her husband was alive and recovering from his injuries in a hospital in Hawaii. Once ambulatory, he was sent home to Long Beach to finish his recovery. "The following year, they sent him out again," said Joan. "That was hard."

He shipped out to New Guinea but didn't fly much because the injuries he sustained made it difficult for him to climb up the ladder into the cockpit. By war's end, Robbie was back in Long Beach Hospital because he was still having trouble with his legs. While he was there, Joan also ended up in the same hospital, but for a happy reason. She gave birth to their daughter, Gail, in September 1945.

After his discharge from the Navy, Robbie resumed his education at USC, eventually earning a doctorate in Education Administration and Philosophy. "It wasn't 'til I received my doctorate that I got to attend my own graduation!" He also joined a Naval Reserve squadron, which didn't please Joan a bit. "I was done with the flying!" she said.

Their son Franklin arrived in 1947, and fifteen years later, daughter Dana completed their family. The couple built a home in North Hollywood, and Robbie launched his teaching career. Over the years, he served as coach, teacher, assistant principal and principal. Eventually, he was asked to open a new secondary school in Beverly Hills. He chronicled his adventures in his second book, *Beverly Hills Principal*.

"We started with 1,000 students and ended up with 4,000," he recalled. "I worked 15 years there on a 10-year contract." He loved his years in public education and worked hard to make a difference during the turbulent times of the 1960's.

At the height of his professional career, Robbie embarked on a new adventure—one that involved his wife. Joan had been working as an administrator of the extension program at Fuller Theological Seminary when they received a call from Texas. "We were asked by the H.E. Butt Foundation to build a continuing education program for the laity," Robbie recalled. "Joan and I worked together for the first time." Though it was hard to leave his position as principal of Beverly Hills High School, the couple decided the time was right to make a change, and off to Texas they went.

"It was a wonderful thing," he said of their time there.

Eventually, they returned to California and built a home on Robbie's family's ranch. This was quite a change for Joan. "I've been a city girl all my life," she said. But she knew how much living at the ranch meant to her husband. Eight years later, Joan suffered heart problems and their time on the ranch came to an end. It was time to explore a new state—Idaho. Their son Franklin pastored the Boise Vineyard Church and urged them to join him in Boise.

As they reflected on their lifetime of love, Joan didn't shy away from the hardships they've endured. "I don't think we'd be the people we are if we hadn't gone through the trials and tribulations we did. It provides a richness that wouldn't be there otherwise."

Robbie sighed and said, "Ours is a deep love that never falters."

LOVE LESSON
"You just have to love each other a whole lot."—Joan Robinson

---

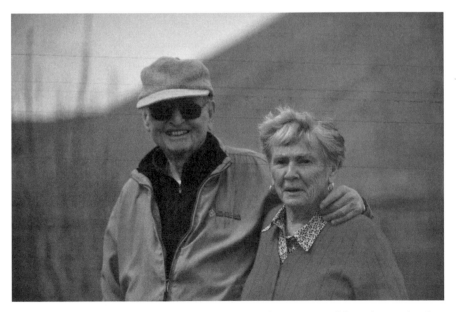

JOAN AND ROBBIE ROBINSON, 2014. *Photo courtesy of the Robinson family*

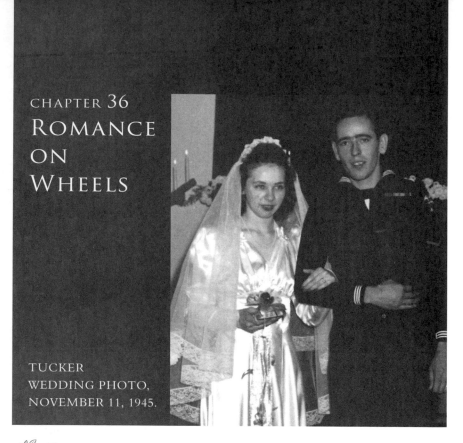

CHAPTER 36
ROMANCE
ON
WHEELS

TUCKER
WEDDING PHOTO,
NOVEMBER 11, 1945.

🌿 *Always*—IRVING BERLIN, 1925

During the 1940s and '50s, many lasting love stories began in a roller rink. That's just what happened to Harold "Tom" Tucker and his bride, Shirley. "I was a sailor stationed at Farragut Naval Training Station," Tom said. "I got liberty and came into Spokane to roller skate."

It was April 1944 and he and other sailors on leave often took a bus to Cook's Roller Rink. Shirley, 17, was a senior at North Central High School. When she skated past, Tom noticed. "I saw her and I thought, WOW! I gotta meet that lady!" They skated together, but Shirley wasn't swept off her feet. She shrugged. "He was alright."

Tom laughed. "She just liked sailors," he teased.

"Oh stop that!" she retorted.

An avid skater, the roller rink was Shirley's favorite place to go. She was there several times a week. "It only cost 35 cents!" A few weeks later Tom showed up at Cook's again and quickly sought her out. This time he asked for her address and phone number. They skated every couples skate together

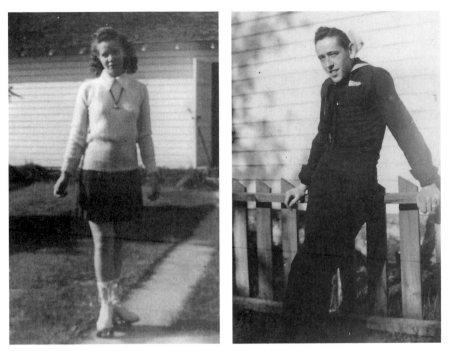

Left: SHIRLEY CAMPBELL IN SKATES JUST PRIOR TO
HER MARRIAGE TO TOM TUCKER, NOVEMBER 1945.
Right: TOM SHORTLY AFTER MEETING SHIRLEY, MAY 1944.

and held hands. "Oh boy! That was fun!" Shirley said. Her parents weren't
thrilled about her dating a sailor, but they figured the youthful romance
would quickly blow over.

It didn't.

After skating, Tom would walk her home from the bus stop, often.
They'd often pause and sit on a wooden fence that surrounded a sand pit.
"That's where I kissed her for the first time," said Tom. "The wind came up
and blew my hat off. Down it went, into the sand pit. She's a powerful kisser
to blow my hat right off!"

In August, Tom asked her father for Shirley's hand in marriage. "I was
madly in love by then," she said. Her father's response? "Absolutely not!
You are both too young." Shirley was heartbroken, knowing Tom would
soon be sent overseas.

"I cried and cried," she said. But her father held firm and when Tom
shipped out for the South Pacific, she didn't have a ring on her finger. A

flurry of letters ensued, but the first one Shirley received puzzled her. "It was from 'Harold' Tucker," she said. "I didn't know any Harold Tuckers!" It seems his fellow sailors at Farragut had christened her beau Tom, as in the nursery rhyme "Little Tommy Tucker," and the name stuck. With that mystery cleared up, Shirley anxiously awaited his missives.

One day a letter arrived and with it came an engagement ring.

"My folks didn't say anything that time," Shirley said. "They could see it was serious." Also serious was the trauma that Tom was about to endure. The 19-year-old hospital corpsman was stationed aboard the USS *LaGrange* and anchored at Buckner Bay near Okinawa.

One night, 13 Japanese twin-engine bombers attacked.

"They hit every ship around us, but didn't hit us," said Tom. "We were young. We stood on the fantail and cheered the anti-aircraft fire. We hollered every time they shot down a plane." Then on August 13, 1945, two days before the war ended, the *LaGrange* was attacked by two kamikaze pilots. One plane struck the ship and damaged it before crashing into the water. The

Left: TOM AND SHIRLEY DATING, AUGUST 1944. *Right:* TOM AND FRIENDS FROM FARRAGUT WITH SHIRLEY'S MOM, AUGUST 1944. (THIS PHOTO WAS ONE TOM RECOVERED FROM THE BAY AFTER THE ATTACK ON THE USS *LaGRANGE*).

other, carrying a bomb, plunged through three decks before the bomb det-onated.

"I was in the dental office trying to write a letter to Shirley," Tom said. "I couldn't think of anything to say, so I went to the mess hall to watch a movie. Five minutes later, the bomb went right through the dental office. The next morning I found my belongings floating in the water." In the fol-lowing hours, Tom did his best to care for the wounded and dying.

"There was fire on the deck—so many men were badly burned. One guy asked for water. I gave him a sip and held his head while he drank. The back of his head came off in my hand. He died 30 minutes later," said Tom.

Another sailor's head had been split in half. Grimly, Tom put the pieces together so the man could be identified. Glancing at her husband, Shirley said, "People really don't know what these guys went through at 18 and 19." The event so shook Tom that he wrote Shirley a letter saying, "Forget about the wedding. We're not getting married."

Stunned, Shirley wept bitterly. Her father cautioned her to wait before replying. She recalled, "He said, 'You wait before you reply. Wait until you're not so upset.'" She listened to his advice and was glad she did because soon another letter from Tom arrived. This one apologized for his earlier note and asked her to make wed-ding plans.

On November 11, 1945, while on a 30-day leave, Tom and Shirley were married. They took a honeymoon trip to Illinois so Shirley could meet his family. However, Tom had to take a train back to his duty sta-tion, meaning Shirley must return to Wash-ington, alone. "I was terrified," she said. "I'd never been anywhere by myself!" A kindly porter watched over her and she made it home safely. Like many newlyweds at the time, the couple spent the first six months of married life living apart. When Tom was discharged in the spring of 1946, he joined

THE TUCKERS ON THEIR HONEYMOON IN ILLINOIS, NOVEMBER 1945.

her in Spokane. But he wasn't sure he wanted to stay in the area. He told Shirley, "I want to go home." He'd had a hard time adjusting to the Pacific Northwest. "I thought I was in prison," he said. "I couldn't see because of the big trees and mountains!"

So off to Illinois they went. However, after a few months Tom turned his bride and said, "Honey, I want to go home." This time home meant Spokane.

Their family quickly grew with the birth of three children; Douglas in 1947, Ronald in 1949 and Pattie in 1951. In 1950, Tom joined the police department and was assigned to the motorcycle unit. He soon found out why motorcycle officers got hazard pay. While responding to a fire, Tom was struck by a car. "We didn't wear helmets back then," he said. "They didn't know if I was going to live for three days." A patrol car picked Shirley up to take her to the hospital and unfortunately, drove right past the accident scene. The sight of her husband's wrecked motorcycle is something she's never forgotten. But Tom recovered and six months later he was back on motorcycle patrol.

After 25 years on the force, Tom retired and then took a job as an investigator for the state Department of Revenue. He was also very active in the Masonic Lodge, and in his 60s became an ordained minister, serving for a time as interim pastor of a local church.

Left: SHIRLEY STILL HAS THE SKATES SHE WORE THE DAY SHE AND TOM MET. *Right:* TOM'S SOUVENIRS FROM THE ATTACK ON THE USS *LAGRANGE*.

For 69 years, the Tuckers supported and encouraged each other. "We talk about everything and make all our decisions together," said Shirley. "He has always been there for me—always."

Perhaps it's no coincidence that the name of "their song" is *Always*. It was sung at their wedding and played at their 50th anniversary. Smiling at the memory, Tom sang, "I'll be loving you, always . . ."

He looked across the room at the girl he first saw at the roller rink so many years ago and said, "She's the other half of me."

LOVE LESSON

"Be supportive of each other's interests. Tom doesn't like to dig in the dirt, but I love to garden and he comes out there and weeds with me."—Shirley Tucker

---

SHIRLEY AND TOM TUCKER, DECEMBER 2014.

AFTERWORD

In the course of writing *War Bonds,* I interviewed close to 50 couples who've been together 60 to 70-plus years.

I found myself searching for a common thread. What is the magic that draws two people together and then keeps them together—through war, through peace, through tragedy, through triumph? What is the secret tie that binds?

It could be as simple as this: when most of these couples married (1938–1950), divorce was still relatively uncommon and society frowned upon it.

It could be that many of the couples shared a commitment to a religious faith that forbade breaking the marriage covenant.

It could be that until the equal rights movement of the 1960's and 70's, many women stayed in marriages because they felt unable to define themselves without husband or children.

Certainly all of these aspects factored in.

However, out of the 36 couples featured in this book, not all of them shared a religious faith. Many of the women enjoyed rewarding careers outside the home, and all of the couples were around when "no-fault divorce" became the norm. Though their stories are filled with the kind of romantic love that many of us aspire to, these weren't perfect marriages. These couples experienced heartache, hardship, bickering, loss, monetary worries and health issues. In sifting through these stories, I found several qualities the couples shared.

Friendship. Simply put, they really liked each other. While passion and romance ebbed and flowed, their enjoyment of each other's company remained.

Respect. Both partners valued what their spouses brought to the marriage and championed their individual talents.

Commitment. One bride said, "After 50 years together, the memories

213

of the bad times pale in comparison to all they joys you've shared and it gives you hope that you can keep on making more happy memories."

Lastly, in spite of what was going on in the world when these couples met and married, they exhibited relentless optimism. They believed in causes bigger than themselves. They felt like what they did mattered—whether it was fighting Hitler overseas, or planting Victory Gardens at home.

When the war ended they formed their marriages and families the same way—with optimism, resiliency and courage. And those of us who are reaping the benefits of their wisdom and sacrifice owe them a debt of gratitude.

Greatest Generation, indeed.